SO YOU THINK YOU'RE A CLEVELAND BROWNS FAN?

STARS, STATS, RECORDS, AND MEMORIES FOR TRUE DIEHARDS

ROGER GORDON
FOREWORD BY THOM DARDEN

SPORTS PUBLISHING

Visit our website at www.sportspubbooks.com.

10 9 8 7 6 5 4 3

Library of Congress Cataloging-in-Publication Data is available on file.

Cover design by Tom Lau
Cover photo credit Associated Press

ISBN: 978-1-68358-098-0
Ebook ISBN: 978-1-68358-102-4

Printed in China

Contents

Foreword

Everyone knows about Babe Ruth's illustrious "called shot" home run during Game 3 of the 1932 World Series at Wrigley Field. Everybody is familiar with Joe Namath's memorable "guarantee" three days before leading the New York Jets to victory in Super Bowl III. Although on a much smaller scale, I own a modest piece of the "guarantee-gone-good" pie. The date was September 23, 1979. I was hosting my weekly radio show, "All-Pro Jazz," on "The Buzzard," the legendary WMMS-FM 100.7. The next evening, we, recently dubbed the "Kardiac Kids" due to three nail-biting wins to start the season, would take an unblemished 3-0 record into a *Monday Night Football* clash with the also unbeaten, and heavily favored, Dallas Cowboys—"America's Team"—in mammoth Cleveland Stadium.

My guest on the radio show that night before the game was none other than Howard Cosell, who, along with Frank Gifford and "Dandy" Don Meredith, would call the game for ABC. I made a prediction to the living legend on air. I told him, "Howard, I'm gonna intercept a pass tomorrow night."

That was quite a bold statement I made. After all, Dallas quarterback Roger Staubach had not thrown a pick in his last 154 passes dating back to the previous season. But the next evening, with us already leading 13-0 early on and the Cowboys at their own 35-yard line in front of more than 80,000 howling fans, Roger "The Dodger," out of his usual shotgun formation, fired a pass over the middle intended for Ron Springs. I stepped in front of the Dallas running back, intercepted the ball, and returned it 39 yards for a touchdown that not only upped our lead to 20-zip before the Cowboys had gained even a single first down, but also brought the huge stadium to a deafening din. That place was rockin'! The electricity in the stadium that night was unbelievable. It was certainly one of my finer moments. To top things off, after the pick-six, Cosell told the entire nation about my prophecy the previous evening. We went on to beat Dallas 26-7.

Another reason I will never forget that momentous interception I made? I grew up a Browns fan. I was born and raised in Sandusky, a little more than an hour west of Cleveland. I was ecstatic when they selected me in the first round of the 1972 draft out of the University of Michigan.

From my rookie season in 1972 when in the playoffs we nearly upset the soon-to-be undefeated Super Bowl Champion Miami Dolphins, to the unforgettable Kardiac Kids days toward the end of my career, I cherished my time as a Cleveland Brown—even the down years. Playing in front of those loyal fans in that huge, old stadium was quite a thrill.

Speaking of thrills, *So You Think You're a Cleveland Browns Fan?* is full of them, along with some heartbreaking memories as well. Browns fans new and old will enjoy flipping the pages from beginning to end while either reliving, or learning about, historical players, coaches, games, and much, much more.

I can only hope success is right around the corner for the present Browns. In fact, because I seem to be such a gifted prognosticator, almost forty years after my fearless forecast rang true against the Cowboys, I'm going to give it another shot: The Browns will win the Super Bowl by 2020. No fans deserve it more than Cleveland fans.

—Thom Darden
*Safety, Cleveland Browns, 1972-74, 1976-81

Preface

I'm embarrassed, ashamed even, to admit that on the afternoon of January 4, 1981, I was rooting for the Browns to lose—yes, LOSE!—to the Oakland Raiders. It was the "Red Right 88" game, the infamous AFC Divisional "Polar" Playoff in Cleveland. The Browns lost a heartbreaker 14-12 when Mike Davis intercepted a pass by Brian Sipe with less than a minute to go. Davis's pick closed the book on what had been a thrill-a-minute Kardiac Kids season for Cleveland. The Raiders went on to win Super Bowl XV.

From the time I was nine years old, I had taken after my older brother Bruce and rooted for the Cleveland Indians and Cleveland Cavaliers. But, for some reason, Bruce would not become a Browns fan until a couple of years later, leaving me without an NFL team for which to root. Early in the 1976 season I decided that I needed to have a favorite pro football team. I thought "Oakland Raiders" sounded really cool. I also liked their silver and black colors. I came to idolize quarterback Ken "The Snake" Stabler, who remains my all-time favorite athlete.

I was on cloud nine when Oakland won the Super Bowl in that 1976 season and almost returned to the Big Game the next year. While the Raiders missed the playoffs in 1978 and 1979, Bruce was becoming a big Browns fan. He and I would argue about who was better, the Browns or the Raiders, Sipe or Stabler (who actually had been traded by Oakland prior to the

1980 season). It was an ongoing battle, especially on days when the league statistics were published in the newspaper.

"Sipe's got more touchdown passes," Bruce would say, doing his best to irritate me.

"Yeah, he's also got more interceptions," I would retaliate.

Our little family feud came to a crashing climax the Sunday of the 1981 Browns-Raiders game, an afternoon in which Northeast Ohio, along with the entire northeastern region of the country, was in a deep freeze. The tension inside 907 Twenty-fourth Street NE in Canton likely rivaled that inside enormous Cleveland Stadium some 60 miles to the north, where the wind chill made the one-degree temperature feel like minus-37 at game time.

Not only were Bruce (who was home from college for winter break) and I on opposite ends of the rooting spectrum, we were on opposite ends of the house that day, me upstairs in our bedroom, him in the basement. Had we watched NBC's telecast together, it would have been not only an unpleasant situation but quite possibly an unhealthy one. The scene could have turned ugly—especially for me—due to the final result. My brother, five years my senior, could have inflicted serious damage on my frail thirteen-year-old body.

The game was not surprisingly a defensive struggle. With little more than two minutes left, Oakland was up by two points and had a fourth down and a yard to go for a first down deep in Browns territory. The Raiders chose to eschew a field-goal try and instead went for the clincher. All they had to do was gain one yard—actually, less than that . . . inches—and the game, for all intents and purposes, would be over. The much-maligned Cleveland defense stopped Oakland, though, and the Browns gained possession of the ball on their own 15-yard line.

Sipe, the NFL MVP in 1980 elected by both the Pro Football Writers Association and *The Sporting News*, drove his team to the Raiders' 13-yard line in what the entire city of Cleveland hoped would turn out to be yet another Kardiac victory. The Browns called timeout with 49 seconds remaining. By this time, my nerves were gripping me. This tension, though, was different than most kinds. Here it was, with less than a minute to go, my beloved Raiders up by two, and . . . *he'll kill me if the Browns lose.* Football clearly wasn't the only thing on my mind. Knowing full well Bruce would be in a nasty mood if the Browns lost, and even more so since he knew I was pulling for the Raiders (or was I?), decision time had arrived. It boiled down to this: If the Browns won, my team would have been eliminated but I'd live; if the Raiders won, my team would have advanced to the AFC Championship game a week later in San Diego, but I might not have been around to see it. After Sipe's errant pass, I was numb, terrified to leave the room. I was unsure of my emotions. I did know one thing, though—silence was the word of the day.

I have come a long way since that fateful, freezing afternoon in the winter of 1981. With Stabler long gone from the silver and black and the Raiders having relocated to Los Angeles, by December 1982 I had become a full-fledged Browns fan. From "The Drive" to "The Fumble" to "The Move" to the reincarnation of the team in 1999, and to the horror show the franchise has been ever since, I have remained loyal to the orange and brown. In fact, I've become so loyal that when I was presented with the opportunity to write *So You Think You're a Cleveland Browns Fan?*, I couldn't resist. Hopefully, this book—in which I present a grab bag of 100 trivia questions and answers that become more difficult with each passing chapter—will test your knowledge when it comes to the history of this fabled franchise. From Otto Graham's exceptional exploits to Jim Brown's greatness to the first *Monday Night Football* game to Tim Couch's two Hail Mary prayers answered, it's all here.

Perhaps one of these days the Browns will play in a Super Bowl. I know, I know, first they have to find a quarterback. Then they have to surround that quarterback with some talent. Finally, they must qualify for the postseason, something they haven't done in 15 years. Then, at least, they'll have a shot. If they do make the playoffs, however, chances are they'll lose in heartbreaking fashion, not unlike the Red Right 88 defeat to the Raiders and the agonizing postseason defeats that followed.

If that happens, at least this time I'd be sure of my emotions . . . *how do I get to the 480 Bridge?*

PRACTICE SQUAD LEVEL

Even if you're just a casual Browns fan, you should have no problem answering these 25 questions correctly. Ready, se-e-e-et, hike!

1. Bernie Kosar was a first-round selection in the 1986 supplemental draft. True or false? *Answer on page 5.*

2. I was the first player ever signed by the Browns. I attended Northwestern University and quarterbacked Cleveland to 10 straight championship games from 1946-55. Who am I? *Answer on page 7.*

3. The Browns were members of the _____ from 1946-49. *Answer on page 8.*
   a. All-America Football League
   b. All-American Football Conference
   c. All-National Football Conference
   d. All-America Football Conference

4. What three seasons was the city of Cleveland without the Browns after they relocated to Baltimore? *Answer on page 10.*

5. The first head coach of the Browns was _____. *Answer on page 10.*

6. Eric Metcalf returned two punts for touchdowns in a 28-23 victory over the _____ on October 24, 1993, in Cleveland Stadium. *Answer on page 11.*

7. Match the head coaches on the left with the years they coached on the right. *Answer on page 14.*

Nick Skorich	1984-88
Butch Davis	1975-77
Marty Schottenheimer	1971-74
Forrest Gregg	2001-04

8. I was a 13th-round draft pick in 1972 from San Diego State University. I passed for 4,132 yards in leading the Browns to the 1980 AFC Central Division title. Who am I? *Answer on page 16.*

9. What running back from Syracuse University, who would spend nine remarkable seasons with the Browns, did the team select in the first round of the 1957 draft? *Answer on page 18.*

10. I quarterbacked the Browns to the 1964 NFL Championship. Who am I? *Answer on page 19.*

11. When the Browns became members of the AFC Central Division in 1970, what were the other three teams in the division? *Answer on page 20.*
   a. Pittsburgh, Cincinnati, Buffalo
   b. Cincinnati, Houston, Pittsburgh
   c. Pittsburgh, Baltimore, Cincinnati
   d. Houston, Baltimore, Pittsburgh

12. The Browns shut out the _____ 27-0 in the 1964 NFL Championship game. *Answer on page 22.*

13. What University of Kentucky quarterback did the Browns select with the No. 1 overall pick in the 1999 draft? *Answer on page 23.*

14. The Browns defeated the New York _____ 31-21 on September 21, 1970, in the first *Monday Night Football* game on ABC in front of a Browns home-record 85,703 fans. *Answer on page 25.*

15. What current AFC North team embarrassed the Browns 43-0 in their nationally televised expansion debut on September 12, 1999, in Cleveland Browns Stadium? *Answer on page 25.*

16. From what university did 2005 draft choice Charlie Frye come? *Answer on page 26.*
   a. Kent State University
   b. University of Toledo
   c. University of Cincinnati
   d. University of Akron

17. What former New York Giants defensive coordinator was the Browns head coach from 1991-95? *Answer on page 28.*

18. What current NFC North team did the Browns oppose in the NFL Championship game four times in the 1950s? *Answer on page 29.*

19. I was chosen with the third overall pick in the 1970 draft after the Browns traded Paul Warfield to the Miami Dolphins for the right to draft me. I had starred as a quarterback at Purdue University from 1967-69. Who am I? *Answer on page 32.*

20. Chris Palmer was the Browns' head coach from 1999-2001. True or false? *Answer on page 33.*

21. The Browns crushed the Pittsburgh Steelers in the 1989 season opener at Three Rivers Stadium by the score of _____. *Answer on page 33.*

    a. 31-0   b. 41-0

    c. 51-0   d. 61-0

22. I am the Browns' all-time leader in receptions with 662. Who am I? *Answer on page 34.*

23. To what team did the Browns lose three AFC Championship games in 1986, 1987, and 1989? *Answer on page 35.*

24. What quarterback with the initials B.N. led the Browns to NFL title-game appearances in 1968 and 1969? *Answer on page 38.*

25. What Boston College product with the initials W.G. led the Browns in rushing yards and rushing touchdowns in his rookie season of 2002? *Answer on page 40.*

PRACTICE SQUAD
LEVEL – ANSWERS

1. False. The Browns chose Kosar in the first round of the 1985 supplemental draft out of the University of Miami. They had traded with Buffalo for the rights to draft him. He had gone public with his desire to play for the Browns, the team he rooted for while growing up in nearby Boardman.

Kosar fumbled his first snap in a home game against New England on October 6, 1985, after starter Gary Danielson was injured in the second quarter. However, he completed his first seven passes en route to a 24-20 victory. He and the oft-injured Danielson, who had been traded from the Lions during the off-season to stand in for the rookie until he was ready, shared the starting duties as the Browns won the AFC Central Division title despite an 8-8 record. In a divisional playoff they squandered a huge lead and, with Kosar passing for just 66 yards in a run-oriented attack, lost 24-21 to the heavily favored Dolphins in Miami.

It took a while, but new offensive coordinator Lindy Infante opened up the offense in 1986. Kosar's true coming-out party occurred when he threw for 401 yards in a Monday night revenge win over the Dolphins. Two weeks later he hung up 414 yards in a 37-31 overtime win against the visiting Steelers. With Kosar passing for a career-high 3,854 yards, the Browns finished 12-4 and won the AFC Central again. He engineered an incredible comeback victory at home over the New York Jets in the divisional playoffs by passing for an NFL playoff record 489 yards.

Kosar and the Browns fell to the Denver Broncos a week later in the AFC Championship in "The Drive" game. Kosar had his finest season—his only Pro Bowl year—in 1987, throwing 22 touchdown passes and just 9 interceptions in 12 games and leading the AFC with a 95.4 passer rating. He and his teammates again advanced to the conference title game but again lost to the Broncos in "The Fumble" contest.

Kosar suffered an arm injury in the 1988 season opener at Kansas City, which sidelined him until he made a triumphant return in a Week 8 win over the Cardinals at Phoenix. He got injured again—this time the left knee, ending his

Bernie Kosar. (AndersonsClevelandDesign.com)

season—during a December Monday night loss to the Dolphins in Miami. Despite fighting a late-season arm injury, he led the Browns back to the AFC title game in 1989, but they fell to the Broncos again. Kosar struggled—and was even benched for a game— along with the team in a disastrous 3-13 1990 season, but he rebounded with a solid season the next year, Bill Belichick's first as head coach. The Browns finished just 6-10, though. A broken foot caused Kosar to miss more than half of the 1992 season that ended with a 7-9 record. After playing musical quarterbacks with ex-college teammate Vinny Testaverde during the first half of the 1993 season, and with tensions bubbling over between himself and Belichick, Kosar was released on November 8 of that year. In his nine seasons, he completed 1,853 of 3,150 passes for 21,904 yards with 116 touchdowns and 81 interceptions.

2. Otto Graham. I signed as a free agent and led the Browns to four AAFC championships from 1946-49 and to six NFL championship games from 1950-55, three of which we won. We defeated the New York Yankees 14-9 for the AAFC title in 1946 in Cleveland. The winning score came on a 16-yard touchdown pass from myself to Dante Lavelli late in the game. We beat the Yankees again, this time 14-3, for the 1947 AAFC championship in Yankee Stadium. We finished 14-0 in 1948 and buried Buffalo 49-7 for the conference title. We went 9-1-2 in 1949, beat the visiting Bills in a playoff and defeated San Francisco 21-7, again at home, for the title.

Although I was not the starter in the Browns' very first game, my first four seasons went extremely well. I threw 86 touchdown passes and just 41 interceptions from 1946-49 and won the AAFC passing title three times. It wasn't quite as easy, but I continued my prowess upon the Browns entering the NFL in 1950. In the league championship game that year, I threw four touchdown passes in leading my team past the visiting Los Angeles Rams 30-28, a contest in which we battled back from an eight-point deficit late in the game.

I continued to pass the Browns to victory after victory the next three seasons, but we fell short in the championship game each year, the Rams the culprits in the first year and the Detroit Lions the culprits in the last two. I led the Browns to their second and third NFL titles in 1954 and 1955. We routed Detroit 56-10 in the 1954 game at Cleveland and did the same to the Rams by a 38-14 score at Los Angeles in 1955. Against the Lions I passed for three touchdowns and rushed for three. Against the Rams I threw for two touchdowns and ran for two. I retired after the season. Overall, I completed 1,464 of 2,626 passes for 23,584 yards with 174 touchdowns and 135 interceptions. I was a Pro Bowler from 1950-54. I was inducted into the Pro Football Hall of Fame in 1965.

3. d. All-America Football Conference. They were in the Western Division, which also originally consisted of the Chicago Rockets, Los Angeles Dons, and San Francisco 49ers. The Eastern Division originally consisted of the Brooklyn Dodgers, Buffalo Bisons, Miami Seahawks, and New York Yankees.

It was a sign of things to come when, in their very first game on September 6, 1946, in Cleveland Municipal Stadium, the Browns annihilated Miami 44-0. Including the postseason, the Browns would go on to finish with a four-year AAFC record of 52-4-3, a winning percentage of .907.

Browns in action, 1946. (The Cleveland Press Collection, Michael Schwartz Library, Cleveland State University)

In that first season of 1946 the Browns posted four shut-outs and concluded the regular season with a 66-14 blowout of Brooklyn at Ebbets Field to win the Western Division with a 12-2 record. They beat the New York Yankees 14-9 for the AAFC title in Cleveland, with the winning score coming on a 16-yard touchdown pass from Otto Graham to Dante Lavelli late in the game. The next season the Browns rolled again, winning the Western Division with a 12-1-1 record and defeating the Yankees again 14-3, this time in Yankee Stadium, for the championship. The Browns outdid themselves the following season by winning the Western Division crown with a perfect 14-0 record. They routed the Buffalo Bills 49-7 in Cleveland for their third consecutive conference crown.

With the AAFC down to seven teams and the two-division format scratched, in 1949 the Browns finished 9-1-2, including a 61-14 destruction of the Dons at Los Angeles, and in first place. They beat the fourth-place Bills 31-21 in a playoff at home after tying them twice during the regular season. A week later, again at home, they wrapped up their fourth straight—and the AAFC's last—conference title by defeating the 49ers 21-7.

4. 1996-98. On June 12, 1996, the city of Cleveland and the NFL announced terms of a historic public-private partnership that would continue the Browns franchise and guarantee a new state-of-the-art stadium in Cleveland in 1999. On March 23, 1998, at a league meeting in Orlando, Florida, NFL owners agreed that the Cleveland Browns would be an expansion team in 1999. On September 8, 1998, the NFL awarded majority ownership of the franchise to Al Lerner.

The Browns did not have much time, but they spent months putting together a team through free agency, the expansion draft, and the regular draft, the latter in which University of Kentucky standout quarterback Tim Couch was their top pick and the first overall selection.

5. Paul Brown. Brown held the position from 1946-62. He is the only NFL coach after whom a team has been named. He led Cleveland to four straight championships in the AAFC from 1946-49 and six consecutive title-game appearances in the NFL from 1950-55, three of which his team won—in 1950, 1954, and 1955. His last title-game appearance was in 1957.

An innovator when it came to the game of football, Brown was the first head coach to hire a full-time coaching staff, utilize classroom study to such a broad extent, use intelligence tests, grade his players from individual film clips, and develop a messenger-guard system so he could call plays from the sideline. He had much to do in inventing, or improving, plays such as the screen pass, draw play, and trap plays. He also invented the first single-bar facemask.

Brown's days as head football coach and athletic officer at the Great Lakes Naval Training Center had much to do with his firing by Art Modell on January 9, 1963. Toward the end of his reign as head coach, many players were growing tired of his military-like approach. They also believed the game was passing him by, that his play-calling had become too conservative for the changing times. He was constantly in disagreement with Modell over how the team should be run. His overall record was 158-48-8. He was inducted into the Pro Football Hall of Fame in 1967.

6. Pittsburgh Steelers. This was a battle for the AFC Central Division lead as both the host Browns and Steelers entered the game with 4-2 records. With the Browns leading 7-0 in the second quarter, Metcalf returned a Mark Royals punt 91 yards for a touchdown. By the time there were less than two-and-a-half minutes to go in the game, the Steelers had forged ahead 23-21. Metcalf received another Royals punt and raced down the right sideline for an electrifying 75-yard return for the winning touchdown, bringing the house down in becoming the first player in NFL history to return two punts for touchdowns of 75 yards or more in the same game. Metcalf's gem turned out to be the last truly thrilling moment in Cleveland Stadium, which would be demolished three years later.

Although his claim to fame came as a return man, Metcalf was used out of the backfield as well. He inherited many of the skills his father Terry possessed as a superb running back and return man himself in the 1970s and early 1980s. The younger Metcalf was Cleveland's first selection—the 13th overall pick—in the 1989 NFL draft. The number "13," however, did not turn out to be unlucky for the former University of Texas Longhorn, who accumulated 1,748 combined net yards in his rookie year of 1989, a season that included several amazing plays.

One occurred in an early-season game at Cincinnati on a Monday night in which Metcalf took a screen pass from Bernie Kosar and jitterbugged his way into the end zone, completely faking out two Bengals defenders along the way. His finest performance of the year may have come on November 5 in Tampa. Late in the first quarter, he turned a simple swing pass from Kosar into a 24-yard touchdown reception in which he side-stepped cornerback Rod Jones before cutting into the end zone, tying the score at seven. Metcalf put the finishing touches on an explosive day all-around for the Browns early in the fourth period with a picturesque 43-yard touchdown run off a fake reverse that gave them a 42-24 lead on the way to a 42-31 victory. On Saturday night, December 23, in a season-ending, nationally televised showdown with the Houston Oilers for the Central Division title in the Astrodome, he took a short pass from Kosar and raced down the right sideline for a 68-yard touchdown, a key play in Cleveland's memorable 24-20 come-from-behind victory.

Metcalf's forte, though, came on special teams, and two weeks after the Oilers game he became the first (and remains the only) Brown to score on a kickoff return in postseason play; he sprinted 90 yards for a third-quarter touchdown in a 34-30 triumph over Buffalo in an AFC Divisional Playoff. He continued to show his brilliance in the return game in the coming years. He returned two kickoffs for touchdowns in 1990—one for 101 yards against the Oilers—and scored on a 75-yard punt return against the Bears two years later before his double whammy against the Steelers in 1993, a year in which he led the NFL in all-purpose yards with 1,932. The next year he burned the Bengals twice on punt returns, scoring on a 92-yarder in a season-opening victory and a 73-yarder that helped seal a 37-13 win on October 23.

Metcalf was traded to the Atlanta Falcons on March 25, 1995, but left behind an indelible mark in his six years in the orange and brown. Overall, he returned 127 punts for 1,341

Eric Metcalf. (AndersonsClevelandDesign.com)

yards with the five touchdowns. He returned 139 kickoffs for 2,806 yards with the two touchdowns. He also had 592 rushes for 2,229 yards with 11 touchdowns and 297 receptions for 2,732 yards with 15 touchdowns. He was a Pro Bowler from 1993-94.

7. Nick Skorich was the Browns' head coach from 1971-74, Butch Davis was their head coach from 2001-04, Marty Schottenheimer was their head coach from 1984-88, and Forrest Gregg was their head coach from 1975-77.

After seven seasons as an assistant coach, Skorich began his tenure as head coach by leading the Browns to a 9-5 record and the AFC Central Division title in 1971. His 1972 team finished 10-4 and qualified for the playoffs as the AFC's wild card entrant. Both years, the Browns were ousted in the divisional playoffs, the latter year a near-miss against the eventual unbeaten Super Bowl Champion Miami Dolphins. The 1973 Browns looked to be headed for the playoffs again until losing their last two games to finish 7-5-2. Skorich's 1974 team fell to 4-10 and last place, the franchise's first losing season in 18 years. He was fired with one game left but finished the season in a loss at Houston. Until Eric Mangini in 2009, he was the only Browns head coach who had prior NFL head-coaching experience (with the Philadelphia Eagles from 1961-63). His overall record was 30-24-2 with the Browns.

Davis, fresh off a successful six-year run as the head coach at the University of Miami, took a team that won five games combined the previous two seasons to a 7-9 record in 2001 and a 9-7 mark and a playoff berth in 2002. The 2002 team blew a 24-7 third-quarter lead and fell 36-33 to the Steelers at Pittsburgh in an AFC Wild Card game. Davis's 2003 Browns fell to

5-11 and his 2004 squad was 3-8 when he resigned Thanksgiving weekend. His overall record was 24-35.

Schottenheimer spent four-and-a-half seasons as defensive coordinator before taking over the head-coaching duties for Sam Rutigliano, who was fired halfway through the 1984 season with the Browns' record 1-7. He led them to a 4-4 finish. They won AFC Central Division titles from 1985-87 and were a wild card team in 1988. They lost heartbreaking playoff games to Miami in 1985 and Houston in 1988, which were sandwiched around excruciating AFC title game defeats—that featured "The Drive" and "the Fumble," respectively—to Denver. Philosophical differences with Art Modell led to his resignation following the 1988 season. His overall record was 44-27.

After spending 1974 as an assistant coach, Gregg in 1975 lost his first nine games en route to a 3-11 last-place finish. The Browns improved to 9-5 after a 1-3 start the next year and had a chance to qualify for the playoffs heading into the final week. They began the 1977 season on fire, winning five of their first seven games before faltering and finishing 6-8 and in last place, prompting Modell to fire Gregg with one

Forrest Gregg watches the game as Mike Phipps hangs his head, 1975. (The Cleveland Press Collection, Michael Schwartz Library, Cleveland State University)

15

game left, although his departure was announced publicly as a resignation. His overall record was 18-23.

8. Brian Sipe. I completed 337 of 554 passes in 1980 and was picked for the Pro Bowl in becoming just the second quarterback in NFL annals to pass for 4,000 yards in one season. I had 30 touchdown passes, which tied San Diego's Dan Fouts for most in the AFC, and just 14 interceptions. I was the league's passing leader with a 91.4 rating. It was a magical Kardiac Kids ride that came to a sudden, unfortunate conclusion when I was intercepted by Mike Davis in Oakland's end zone with less than a minute to go in a 14-12 divisional playoff defeat—Red Right 88—in frozen Cleveland Stadium.

I actually had an inauspicious start to my pro career as I spent two seasons on the practice squad before making the regular roster in 1974. I filled in for interception-prone Mike Phipps on occasion that season and was instrumental in three wins, including a stirring comeback at home against Denver in which I scored twice—the second with 1:56 left—after relieving him in the fourth quarter. I also backed him up the next season.

I replaced Phipps once and for all when the Browns' 1970 first-round draft choice went down with a separated shoulder while we were leading the visiting New York Jets 21-10 early in the second half of the 1976 season opener. I directed the Browns to a victory in that game and went on to complete 178 of 312 passes for 2,113 yards with 17 touchdowns and 14 interceptions, becoming the first Cleveland quarterback in seven years to throw for more touchdowns than picks. We improved to 9-5 after 4-10 and 3-11 finishes the two previous seasons, respectively.

An exclamation point had been added to the fact that I had the starting job all to myself when the 1977 season opened as Phipps had been traded to the Bears during the off-season. With us leading the AFC Central Division at 5-3, I suffered a separated left shoulder in a loss to the Steelers that ended my season. We ended up 6-8 and in last place.

In 1978 the arrival of new head coach Sam Rutigliano meant a more pass-oriented offense. I threw for almost 3,000 yards on 222 completions out of 399 attempts with 21 touchdowns and 15 interceptions as we improved to 8-8 after a 3-0 start. I began to really come into my own the next year when I completed 286 of 535 passes for 3,793 yards with 28 touchdowns, which tied New England's Steve Grogan for the NFL high, but also 26 interceptions. We earned the Kardiac Kids nickname from three miraculous wins to start the year. A late-season letdown caused us to barely miss qualifying for the playoffs with a 9-7 record.

In 1981 I completed 313 of 567 passes for 3,876 yards, but I had just 17 touchdown passes and was picked off 25 times as we fell to 5-11 and last place. I was benched in favor of third-year lefty Paul McDonald after we lost four of our first six games in the strike-shortened 1982 season. I regained my starting job in 1983 and started all but two games. I completed 291 of 496 attempts for 3,566 yards with an AFC-best 26 touchdowns but also 23 interceptions. We were 8-5 and looking good but finished 9-7, just missing the playoffs.

I left the Browns after the 1983 season as a free agent to join Donald Trump's New Jersey Generals of the United States Football League. Overall, I had both a team-record 1,944 completions and 3,439 passes for a club-record 23,713 yards with 154 touchdowns and 149 interceptions.

Brian Sipe. (Andersons-ClevelandDesign.com)

9. Jim Brown. In 1957 Brown won the NFL rushing title with 942 yards, leading Cleveland to the Eastern Conference championship. He would go on to win the rushing crown in eight of his nine seasons.

Brown's rookie year included a 237-yard rushing performance against the Los Angeles Rams, an NFL record that stood for 14 seasons until, ironically, the Rams' Willie Ellison broke it by gaining 247 yards against New Orleans. Brown's remarkable feat was a rookie record until 1997 when Cincinnati's Corey Dillon rung up a 246-yard game against Tennessee.

In 1958 Brown rushed for 1,527 yards, topping the 100-yard mark nine times. Despite his team's rather mediocre records the next three years, his ground yardage totals were still exceptional—1,329, 1,257, and 1,408, respectively. In 1959 he set an NFL record that has since been tied on three occasions for most rushing touchdowns in one game with five on November 1 against Baltimore. Four years later he repeated his feat of four years before by totaling 237 yards in a home game against the Eagles.

After a "fall-off" year in 1962 when he gained "just" 996 yards and failed to win the league rushing title, Brown rebounded big time in 1963. He rushed for a career-high 1,863 yards, nearly doubling his output from the year before, basking in new head coach Blanton Collier's wide-open offensive attack that saw the team win 10 games for the first time in a decade (Collier had replaced the fired Paul Brown).

Brown powered his way to 1,446 yards in 1964, a year in which his 46-yard, third-quarter dash in the NFL Championship game ignited Cleveland's 27-0 upset of the Colts. He racked up 1,544 yards in 1965 as the Browns returned to the title game but were beaten by the Green Bay Packers in a frozen Lambeau Field. The loss to Green Bay, it turned out, was Brown's final performance—at least on the gridiron. The great fullback announced his retirement the following summer, opting for an acting career in the movies.

Brown not only was indescribable as a player but indestructible. He never missed a game, a remarkable accomplishment considering he was the main target of opposing defenses most of the time. Overall, he had both a team-record 12,312 yards rushing and 2,359 carries, averaging an astounding 104.3 yards per game, still an NFL record, and an equally amazing 5.2 yards per carry. He rushed for 106 touchdowns and scored 126 overall. He was a Pro Bowler in all nine seasons and was inducted into the Pro Football Hall of Fame in 1971.

10. Frank Ryan. In that 1964 season I completed 174 of 334 passes for 2,404 yards with 25 touchdowns and 19 interceptions as we won the Eastern Conference title with a 10-3-1 record. Three second-half touchdown passes from myself to Gary Collins for 18, 42, and 51 yards led us to a 27-0 upset of Baltimore in the NFL Championship game.

A quarterback from 1962-68, I was traded from the Los Angeles Rams on July 12, 1962. After sharing the signal-calling duties with Jim Ninowski that year, in 1963 I completed 135 of 256 passes with 25 touchdowns and 13 interceptions in directing the Browns to a 10-4 record and second-place finish in the Eastern Conference. In the season opener at home against the Redskins, I connected with Jim Brown on an 83-yard pass play that went for a touchdown en route to a 37-14 victory.

Two years later, I helped the Browns get off to a fine start by throwing an 80-yard touchdown pass to Walter Roberts in a season-opening win against the Redskins, but this time in Washington. I was instrumental in the team returning to the title game, but we fell 23-12 in the snow and sleet of Green Bay. In 1966 I passed for 2,974 yards with 29 touchdowns and just 14 interceptions. I totaled 367 yards through the air on December 17 in a 38-10 rout of the St. Louis Cardinals. My 2,026 yards passing with 20 touchdown passes (and also 16 interceptions) helped us to a 9-5 record and the Century Division championship in 1967. We were crushed, though, 52-14 by the Cowboys in Dallas for the Eastern Conference title. I was replaced by Bill Nelsen three games into the 1968 season.

I was released on September 9, 1969, some two weeks before the start of the season. In my seven years, I completed 907 of 1,755 passes for 13,361 yards with 134 touchdown passes and 88 interceptions. I was a Pro Bowler from 1964-66.

11. b. Cincinnati, Houston, Pittsburgh. With the American Football League-National Football League merger, the Browns and Steelers, along with Baltimore, joined the old AFL teams in the AFC. The Bengals and Oilers were from the AFL.

In 1970 the Browns began the season 4-2, including a 30-27 victory over ex-Cleveland head coach Paul Brown's Bengals. In just their third year of existence, the Bengals lost six of their first seven games but rebounded to win their last seven games, including a 14-10 triumph over the Browns, to finish 8-6 and win the Central Division title by a game over their 7-7 neighbors to the north. Cincinnati lost at Baltimore 17-0 in the divisional playoffs. The Browns began the 1971 season 4-5 but finished 9-5 in winning the weak Central. Pittsburgh finished second but was only 6-8. The Browns fell to the Colts 20-3 in a divisional playoff at home.

The next year was the start of a historic run by the Steelers, a franchise that had played in only one postseason game in its nearly 40-year history. Pittsburgh won the Central Division with an 11-3 record. The Browns were second at 10-4 and the AFC wild card team. Both the Browns and Steelers were ousted by the eventual, undefeated Super Bowl champion Miami Dolphins in the playoffs—Cleveland in the divisional round and Pittsburgh in the conference title game. That season was the first of eight straight playoff appearances—including seven division titles—by the Steelers. They won four Super Bowls during the stretch—Super Bowls IX, X, XIII, and XIV. Toward the end of their remarkable run came the emergence of Earl Campbell and the "Luv Ya Blue" Oilers. Houston was unable to win the division title during its three-year playoff run from 1978-80 but did manage to advance to the AFC Championship game in 1978 and 1979.

Cleveland's Kardiac Kids won the Central Division in 1980, and Cincinnati won it, and advanced to Super Bowl XVI, in 1981. The Steelers, Bengals, and Browns qualified for the 1982 strike-induced, expanded playoffs, but each lost in the first round. Pittsburgh won the (by then) weak Central in 1983 and 1984, advancing to the AFC Championship game the latter year.

The Bernie Kosar-led Browns qualified for the playoffs from 1985-89, winning the Central Division in four of those years and losing the AFC title game to John Elway's Denver Broncos from 1986-87 and in 1989. The Bengals won the division in 1990, the Oilers won it in 1991 and 1993, and the Steelers won it in 1992, 1994, and 1995 (the latter with the Jacksonville Jaguars involved, in what was their inaugural season). The Steelers subsequently advanced to Super Bowl XXX after the 1995 season, losing to the Dallas Cowboys.

With the Browns having relocated to Baltimore in 1996 to become the Ravens, the Central Division champions in the three seasons in which Cleveland had no professional football team were the Steelers from 1996-97 and the Jaguars in 1998. The Oilers had relocated to Tennessee in 1997 and would become the Titans in 1999. Upon the expansion Browns' return to the NFL in 1999, Jacksonville won the Central title that year with a 14-2 record, Tennessee won it in 2000 with a 13-3 mark, and Pittsburgh won it, also with a 13-3 record, in 2001, which, due to realignment, was the last year of the AFC Central Division.

12. Baltimore Colts. The game was played at Cleveland Municipal Stadium in front of 79,544 fans. The Browns, who won the Eastern Conference with a 10-3-1 record, were heavy underdogs to the John Unitas-led Colts, who easily won the Western Conference with a 12-2 record.

After a scoreless first half, the home team took a 3-0 lead in the third quarter when Lou Groza kicked a 43-yard field goal. That was all the points the Browns would need, but they didn't stop there. Later that quarter Frank Ryan threw an 18-yard touchdown pass to Gary Collins to increase the Browns' lead to

10-0. Ryan connected with Collins again on a 42-yard touchdown strike for a 17-0 lead after three quarters. Groza kicked a 10-yard field goal to up the Browns' lead to 20-0. Ryan and Collins put the icing on the cake with a 51-yard connection for a touchdown for the final score of the game. Pandemonium reigned as thousands of fans rushed the field to celebrate the franchise's fourth NFL title and eighth overall.

Ryan was 11-of-18 for 206 yards with the three touchdowns and one interception. Jim Brown rushed the ball 27 times for 114 yards, including a 46-yard jaunt in the third quarter; he had three receptions for 37 yards. Collins had five receptions for 130 yards with the three touchdowns. Unitas was 12-of-20 for 95 yards with two picks. Lenny Moore had nine carries for 40 yards, and Raymond Berry had three catches for 38 yards.

13. Tim Couch. Couch in 1999 completed 223 of 399 passes for 2,447 yards with 15 touchdowns and 13 interceptions, becoming only the sixth rookie quarterback in the NFL since 1952 to have more touchdown passes than interceptions. He replaced starter Ty Detmer in the fourth quarter of the Browns' season-opening 43-0 loss at home to Pittsburgh on September 12.

Couch gave the Browns their first victory of the "new era" when he completed a 56-yard Hail Mary bomb with no time left that was tipped into the hands of Kevin Johnson as the Browns beat New Orleans 21-16 in the Superdome. Couch left the December 19 home game against Jacksonville in the second quarter with an ankle sprain, causing him to miss the final game of the season the next week against the Colts. He got off to a fine start in 2000 with 259 yards passing in a win over the Bengals and 316 yards through the air in a win over

Pittsburgh as the Browns won two of their first three games. In the Steelers game he connected with Johnson on a 79-yard pass play. However, Couch played in just seven games due to a fractured right thumb suffered in a practice session on October 19.

In 2001 Couch came back strong by completing 272 of 454 passes for 3,040 yards with 17 touchdowns and 21 interceptions. After 2-14 and 3-13 seasons, respectively, in 1999 and 2000, the Browns improved to 7-9 and were thinking playoffs into December. Couch directed three fourth-quarter comeback wins, including a 41-38 thriller at Tennessee on December 30 in which he was 20-of-27 for a career-high 336 yards, including a 78-yarder to Quincy Morgan.

In 2002 Couch missed the first two games due to a preseason injury. Upon his return, he led the Browns to eight wins—including a handful of late-game comebacks—in 14 games as the starter but played only part of the finale at home against the Falcons due to another injury. The Browns qualified for the playoffs, but Couch's injury kept him out of their 36-33 wild card playoff defeat to the Steelers in Pittsburgh in which he was replaced by early-season starter Kelly Holcomb. Couch and Holcomb played musical quarterbacks during a 2003 season in which the Browns finished just 5-11. One of Couch's finest performances ever, though, occurred on October 5 that year when he was 20-of-25 for 208 yards with two touchdowns and an interception in a 33-13 upset of the Steelers at Pittsburgh.

Couch was released after the 2003 season. Overall, he completed 1,025 of 1,714 passes for 11,131 yards with 64 touchdowns and 67 interceptions. Most Browns fans would be shocked to learn that he has the highest career completion percentage in team history at 59.8 (minimum 750 passes).

14. Jets. The Browns took a 7-0 lead in the first quarter when Bill Nelsen threw an eight-yard touchdown pass to Gary Collins. Bo Scott's two-yard touchdown run later in the quarter made the score 14-0. The Jets cut the deficit to 14-7 at halftime on Emerson Boozer's five-yard touchdown run in the second quarter.

Homer Jones brought the house down when he returned the second-half kickoff 94 yards for a touchdown to increase the Browns' lead to 21-7. Boozer's 10-yard touchdown run later in the third quarter made the score 21-14, but Don Cockroft's 27-yard field goal upped Cleveland's lead to 24-14 entering the fourth quarter. Joe Namath fired a 33-yard laser to George Sauer for a touchdown to bring New York within 24-21. Billy Andrews clinched the victory when he made a diving interception of a Namath pass, got up, and returned the ball 25 yards for a touchdown with 35 seconds left.

Nelsen was 12-of-27 for 145 yards with the touchdown. Leroy Kelly had 20 rushes for 62 yards. Milt Morin had five receptions for 90 yards. Namath was 18-of-31 for 298 yards with the touchdown and three interceptions. Matt Snell ran the ball 16 times for 108 yards, while Boozer had 15 carries for 58 yards with the two touchdowns and caught three passes for 38 yards. Sauer had 10 catches for 172 yards, and Don Maynard had four receptions for 69 yards.

15. Pittsburgh Steelers. There was much excitement leading up to the Sunday night game, which was broadcast on ESPN. Because the Browns won two games during the preseason, including one in overtime against the defending NFC Eastern Division champion Dallas Cowboys in the Hall of Fame game, many delusional fans were thinking an 8-8 record, and even a playoff berth, were distinct possibilities.

Those unrealistic thoughts were brought to a screeching halt during the Steelers game. Kordell Stewart got things rolling for the visitors when he scored from a yard out for a 7-0 lead with 5:16 to go in the first quarter. Field goals of 18 and 28 yards by Kris Brown sandwiched a five-yard touchdown pass from Stewart to Richard Huntley to give Pittsburgh a 20-0 halftime lead. Huntley scored on a three-yard touchdown run to up the Steelers' lead to 26-0 entering the fourth quarter. Brown nailed a 19-yard field goal early in the fourth. Soon after, Huntley scored again, this time on a 21-yard touchdown pass from Mike Tomczak. Tomczak hit Hines Ward midway through the final period to nail the coffin door shut on the Browns.

The game was so one-sided that Pittsburgh actually had more points than Cleveland had total yards (40). The Steelers had 464 total yards. They outgained the Browns 217-9 in rushing yards. The Steelers had 33 first downs to the Browns' two. The Browns had four turnovers, the Steelers none. Time of possession? Pittsburgh 47:49, Cleveland 12:11.

Ty Detmer was 6-of-13 for 52 yards with an interception and was sacked twice. Leslie Shepherd had two receptions for 32 yards. Stewart was 15-of-23 for 173 yards with the touchdown and was sacked once. Tomczak was 8-of-8 for 78 yards with the two touchdowns. Jerome Bettis rushed the ball 18 times for 89 yards. Huntley had five catches for 67 yards with the two touchdowns and carried the ball 10 times for 41 yards with the touchdown.

16. d. University of Akron. Frye was chosen in the third round. He backed up Trent Dilfer for most of his 2005 rookie season in which the Browns finished 6-10 and in last place in the AFC North. He completed 98 of 164 passes for 1,002 yards with four touchdowns and five interceptions. His best game was on December 4 at home against Jacksonville when he went 13-of-20 for 226 yards with two touchdowns. However, he was sacked five times and the Browns lost 20-14. Two weeks later at Oakland he engineered a memorable drive that began on the Cleveland 37-yard line with 3:15 to go and ended on a 37-yard field goal by Phil Dawson with no time left that gave the Browns a 9-7 victory.

Frye was the starter when the 2006 season opened. He started all but three games, completing 252 of 393 passes for 2,454 yards with 10 touchdowns and 17 picks as the Browns finished 4-12 and in last place again. He directed another comeback win over the Raiders in Oakland on October 1. With the Browns down 21-3 late in the first half, he completed a three-yard touchdown pass to Darnell Dinkins to cut it to 21-10 at halftime. With 8:03 to go in the third quarter, he capped a 69-yard drive when he connected with Kellen Winslow on a two-yard touchdown strike to make the score 21-17. Later in the quarter the Browns took their only lead of the game when Frye did it again, this time a five-yard touchdown strike to Joe Jurevicius for a 24-21 Cleveland lead. The Browns were able to hang on for the victory.

Frye again was the opening-day starter in 2007, but his atrocious performance—4-of-10 for 34 yards with an interception and five sacks before getting yanked late in the first half—in a 34-7 home loss to Pittsburgh resulted in him getting traded to Seattle two days later, prompting many to observe that they couldn't remember an opening-day NFL starting quarterback being traded after just one game. Overall, he completed 354 of 567 passes for 3,490 yards with 14 touchdowns and 23 interceptions.

17. Bill Belichick. Belichick took over a Browns team coming off a 3-13 1990 season. He was previously the New York Giants' defensive coordinator from 1985-90 and was part of two Super Bowl titles—in 1986 and 1990—during that period. Prior to that, he was the Giants' linebackers and special teams coach from 1980-84 and was their special teams coach and a defensive assistant in 1979. He began his NFL coaching career in 1975 as a special assistant for the Baltimore Colts. He was an assistant for Detroit from 1976-77 and for Denver in 1978.

Under Belichick, the 1991 Browns improved to 6-10. They actually came very close to finishing above .500, for they lost several close games, including a nightmarish stretch in November when they suffered three consecutive crushing defeats by a total of eight points, squandering late-game leads in each. The 1992 Browns began the season 0-2. Bernie Kosar broke his ankle in the second week and missed nine games. With a combination of Todd Philcox and Mike Tomczak calling the signals while Number 19 was out and with Kosar back for the last five games, the Browns got to 7-6 and within sniffing distance of a playoff berth. They lost their last three games, however, to finish 7-9. They won their first three games in 1993 and, after a thrilling win over Pittsburgh, stood at 5-2 and in first place in the AFC Central Division. They were beaten badly by Denver, Kosar got cut, and they finished 7-9 again.

With Vinny Testaverde the main quarterback in 1994, a stout defense led the way to an 11-5 record and a victory over the Patriots in the first round of the playoffs. The Steelers brought the Browns back to Earth in the second round. Belichick's 1995 Browns began 3-1, but three straight losses—including an embarrassing one at home to expansion Jacksonville— followed. Two weeks later Art Modell dropped the bombshell that the Browns would move to Baltimore in 1996. Soon after the 5-11 season he fired Belichick, who wound up with a 36-44 overall record.

18. Detroit Lions. Cleveland and Detroit faced each other for the NFL title from 1952-54 and in 1957. The Lions won from 1952-53 and in 1957, and the Browns won in 1954. In 1952 the Browns, who won the American Conference with an 8-4 record, lost to the Lions 17-7 on December 28 in Cleveland. Bobby Layne gave the visitors a 7-0 lead in the second quarter on a two-yard touchdown run. Detroit, which finished 9-3 and then beat the Rams in a tiebreaker playoff to win the National Conference, upped its lead to 14-0 in the third quarter when Doak Walker busted loose for a 67-yard touchdown. The Browns got on the board when Harry Jagade ran the ball in from seven yards out to make the score 14-7. Pat Harder kicked a 36-yard field goal in the fourth quarter for the game's final points.

Otto Graham was 20-of-35 for 191 yards with an interception. Jagade rushed the ball 15 times for 104 yards with the touchdown, and Marion Motely had six carries for 74 yards, including a 42-yard run, and had three receptions for 21 yards. Darrel Brewster had two receptions for 53 yards, including a 32-yarder from Graham. Layne was 7-of-9 for 68 yards. Walker rushed the ball 10 times for 97 yards.

The next season the Browns, who won the Eastern Conference with an 11-1 record, lost to the Lions 17-16 on December 27 at Detroit. Walker gave the Lions, who won the Western Conference with a 10-2 record, a 7-0 first-quarter lead when he scored from a yard out. The teams traded field goals in the second quarter, and the Lions led 10-3 at the half. Jagade's nine-yard touchdown run in the third quarter tied the game at 10. Two Lou Groza field goals in the fourth quarter put the Browns ahead 16-10, but Layne's 33-yard touchdown pass to Jim Doran gave the Lions the victory.

Graham was just 2-of-15 for 20 yards with two interceptions. Jagade rushed the ball 15 times for 102 yards, including a 30-yarder, and had an 18-yard reception. Layne was 12-of-25 for 179 yards with the touchdown and two picks. Bob Hoernschemeyer had 17 carries for 51 yards, while Doran caught four passes for 95 yards with the touchdown.

In 1954 the Browns, who won the Eastern Conference with a 9-3 record, destroyed the Lions 56-10 on December 26 at Cleveland. After an early field goal by Detroit, which won the Western Conference with a 9-2-1 mark, Graham threw touchdown passes to Ray Renfro and Brewster, respectively, to give the Browns a 14-3 lead after the first quarter. Two short touchdown rushes by Graham plus a 31-yard touchdown strike from Graham to Renfro upped the Cleveland lead to 35-10 at halftime. Three more touchdown runs by the Browns—including another short one by Graham—were the final points in the rout.

Graham was 9-of-12 for 163 yards with the three touchdowns and two interceptions. Chet Hanulak had five rushes for 44 yards with a touchdown. Renfro caught five passes for 94 yards with the two touchdowns. Layne was 18-of-42 for 177 yards with six picks. Lew Carpenter had eight rushes for 64 yards, including a 52-yarder, and Bill Bowman had seven carries for 61 yards with a touchdown. Dorne Dibble had four receptions for 63 yards, while Jug Girard caught five passes for 57 yards.

In 1957 the Lions, who finished 8-4 and then beat the 49ers in a tiebreaker playoff to win the Western Conference, hammered the Browns, who won the Eastern Conference with a 9-2-1 mark, 59-14 on December 29 at Detroit. It was all Lions from the start. A 31-yard field goal by Jim Martin preceded one-yard touchdown runs by Tobin Rote and Gene Gedman to give Detroit a 17-0 lead after one quarter. The Lions increased their lead to 31-7 at halftime and 45-14 after three quarters. They put the icing on the cake in the fourth quarter on touchdown passes from Rote to Dave Middleton and from Jerry Reichow to Howard Cassady.

Milt Plum was 5-of-12 for 51 yards with two interceptions, one of which was a 19-yard return for a touchdown by Terry Barr. Carpenter, by then with the Browns, rushed the ball 14 times for 82 yards with a touchdown. A rookie by the name

Action from the NFL Championship game between the Browns and Lions, December 29, 1957. (The Cleveland Press Collection, Michael Schwartz Library, Cleveland State University)

of Jim Brown had 20 carries for 69 yards with a touchdown. Brewster had three receptions for 52 yards. Rote was 12-of-19 for 280 yards with four touchdowns. Cassady ran the ball eight times for 48 yards and had two catches for 22 yards with the touchdown. Steve Junker had five receptions for 109 yards with two touchdowns, and Doran had three catches for 101 yards, including a 78-yarder for a touchdown from Rote.

19. Mike Phipps. I had led the Boilermakers to 24 victories in 30 games, including a pair of Associated Press top 10 finishes. I did not become the Browns' full-time starter until I replaced veteran Bill Nelsen in Week 2 of the 1972 season. That year was my best—I completed 144 of 305 passes for 1,994 yards with 13 touchdowns and 16 interceptions. We finished 10-4, and despite my 5 interceptions, took the undefeated Dolphins down to the wire in a 20-14 AFC Divisional Playoff defeat in the Orange Bowl.

Things went downhill from there. The following are my touchdown passes/interceptions ratios for the next three seasons: 9/20, 9/17, and 4/19. Our records those years dropped to 7-5-2, 4-10, and 3-11, respectively. I held off a challenge from Brian Sipe in the 1976 training camp and started the opening game against the New York Jets at home. I passed for three second-quarter touchdowns en route to a 21-10 halftime lead only to suffer a separated shoulder early in the third quarter that caused me to miss most of the season. Sipe came in and put the finishing touches on a 38-17 victory. He went on to lead the Browns to a 9-5 record, and the starting job was his. I was traded to the Chicago Bears on May 3, 1977. Overall, I completed 633 of 1,317 passes for the Browns, for 7,700 yards with 40 touchdowns and 81 interceptions.

20. False. Palmer was the head coach from 1999-2000. Under Palmer, the "reborn" Browns took the field for the first time on September 12, 1999, against the Pittsburgh Steelers at brand new Cleveland Browns Stadium in a game broadcast on ESPN. The Browns not only lost 43-0 but were only able to muster two first downs and 40 total yards. As expected, they had a rough time of it that season. They didn't score as many as 20 points in a game until Week 8, which was also their first win, 21-16 at New Orleans on a Hail Mary pass at the end. They finished 2-14 and in last place in the AFC Central.

Palmer's Browns started 2-1 in 2000, but it was downhill from there. They lost four straight games, including a 36-10 rout at Oakland and a 44-10 beating at Denver, to drop to 2-5. Then Tim Couch broke his right thumb in a practice session, ending his season. With castoff Doug Pederson and Spergon Wynn calling the signals the rest of the way, the Browns lost eight of their last nine games, including a 48-0 embarrassment at Jacksonville, to finish 3-13 and in last place again. Palmer was fired after the season. He was 5-27 overall.

21. c. 51-0. The date was September 10, a day that Browns fans will never forget. It was quite a homecoming for Bud Carson. The former Steelers' defensive coordinator, and architect of the famed "Steel Curtain" defense of the 1970s, returned to Pittsburgh for his first game as an NFL head coach.

The Browns humiliated the Steelers. They scored three defensive touchdowns, beginning with Clay Matthews's three-yard fumble return in the first quarter for a 7-0 lead. By the time the first quarter was done, Matt Bahr had kicked a 27-yard field goal and David Grayson had returned a fumble 28 yards for a touchdown, giving Cleveland a 17-0 lead. In the second quarter two Bahr field goals sandwiched a Tim Manoa three-yard touchdown run for a 30-0 lead at the half.

In the third quarter Manoa scored on a two-yard run, and Grayson returned a Bubby Brister pass 14 yards for a touchdown to increase the Browns' lead to 44-0. Even the infamous Mike Oliphant got into the act with a 21-yard touchdown run in the fourth quarter for the final points. What made the rout even more remarkable was that the Browns amassed their points total without scoring in the first 9:18 and last 11:34 of the game, meaning they did all of their damage in just more than a two-and-a-half-quarter period, from late in the first to early in the fourth.

The Browns had 19 first downs to the Steelers' five. They outgained them 357-53 in total yards. They forced eight turnovers while committing none. Bernie Kosar was 16-of-25 for 207 yards and was sacked once. Oliphant had six rushes for 48 yards with the touchdown. Webster Slaughter caught four passes for 75 yards, including a 51-yarder from Kosar. Brister was 10-of-22 for 84 yards with three interceptions; he was sacked six times.

22. Ozzie Newsome. I was a first-round selection out of the University of Alabama in 1978 and a tight end from 1978-90. I got off to a fine start as I scored on a 33-yard end-around in my very first game, a victory over the San Francisco 49ers in Week 1 of the 1978 season. I had 38 receptions for 589 yards with two touchdown catches that year, 55 receptions for 781 yards and nine touchdown catches in 1979, and 51 receptions for 594 yards and three touchdown catches in 1980. I led the Browns in receptions and receiving yards every season from 1981-85 and in touchdown receptions in 1979, 1981, and from 1983-85. My 1,002 yards receiving in 1981 were the most by a Brown in thirteen years.

In the strike-shortened season of 1982 I had 49 receptions for 633 yards with three touchdowns. I amassed a team-record 89 catches (tied by Kellen Winslow in 2006) in both the 1983 and 1984 seasons for 970 and 1,001 yards, respectively. I totaled 191 receiving yards on 14 receptions at home against the New York Jets on October 14, 1984. I caught 62 passes for 711 yards in 1985. I had 114 receiving yards in a 23-20 double-overtime victory over the Jets in an AFC Divisional Playoff on January 3, 1987, in Cleveland.

I retired after the 1990 season. My 662 career receptions are the most in Browns history, as are my 7,980 career receiving yards. I was a Pro Bowler in 1981 and from 1984-85 and was inducted into the Pro Football Hall of Fame in 1999.

23. Denver Broncos. In the Broncos and Browns' first meeting on January 11, 1987, in Cleveland, the Browns, who won the AFC Central with a 12-4 record and had beaten the Jets in the divisional playoffs the week before, got on the board first when in the opening quarter Bernie Kosar completed a six-yard touchdown pass to Herman Fontenot. The Broncos, who won the AFC West with an 11-5 record and had defeated the Patriots in a divisional playoff a week earlier, got on the board in the second quarter on a 19-yard Rich Karlis field goal and then forged ahead 10-7 on a Gerald Willhite one-yard touchdown run. Mark Moseley's 29-yard field goal tied the game 10-10 at halftime.

In the third quarter the teams traded field goals, and then what looked to be the play of the game occurred when Kosar launched one to Brian Brennan for a 48-yard catch-and-run touchdown with 5:43 to go in the game. Brennan caught Kosar's underthrown aerial at the 16-yard line, completely faked out strong safety Dennis Smith, and waltzed into the end zone, giving the Browns what almost 80,000 witnesses believed was a berth in Super Bowl XXI. After a muff by Gene Lang on the ensuing kickoff pinned the Broncos on their own two-yard line, John Elway came to the rescue by directing an improbable 98-yard touchdown drive—including a 20-yard completion to Mark Jackson on a third-and-18 play—to tie the game with 37 seconds left. The final piece of the 15-play march was a five-yard scoring strike from Elway to Jackson. Karlis kicked a 33-yard field goal in overtime—a boot that many Browns players and fans still claim to have been wide left—to give the Broncos a 23-20 triumph.

Kosar was 18-of-32 for 259 yards with the two touchdowns and two interceptions; he was sacked once. Kevin Mack ran the ball 26 times for 94 yards and had two receptions for 20 yards. Brennan had four receptions for 72 yards with the touchdown, and Fontenot had seven catches for 66 yards with the touchdown. Elway was 22-of-38 for 244 yards with the touchdown and a pick and was sacked twice. He ran the ball four times for 56 yards, including a 34-yarder. Sammy Winder rushed the ball 26 times for 83 yards. Steve Watson and Steve Sewell each had three receptions, for 55 yards and 47 yards, respectively.

The Browns and Broncos met again a year later, on January 17, 1988, in the AFC Championship game, this time in Denver. The Broncos, who won the AFC West with a players' strike-induced 10-4-1 record and had beaten Houston in the divisional playoffs the week before, scored first and scored often in the first half. Elway's eight-yard touchdown pass to Ricky

Nattiel and Sewell's one-yard touchdown run gave them a 14-0 lead after one quarter. By halftime the score was 21-3. Kosar hit Reggie Langhorne on an 18-yard scoring strike to make it 21-10 in the third quarter. Soon after, however, Jackson caught a short pass from Elway and raced down the right sideline for an 80-yard touchdown to make it 28-10, seemingly thrusting a knife into the visitors' collective heart.

But the Browns, who won the AFC Central with a 10-5 record and had beaten the Colts a week earlier in a divisional play-off, refused to die. Kosar connected with Byner on a 32-yard touchdown pass, and then Byner scored from 4 yards out as they pulled within 28-24. They trailed 31-24 heading into the fourth quarter before tying the score at 31 when Kosar hit Webster Slaughter on a four-yard touchdown pass. Elway and Winder connected on a 20-yard touchdown strike as Denver took the lead again 38-31. With little more than a minute to go, the Browns were driving again, at Denver's eight-yard line. Byner took a handoff from Kosar, burst off left tackle, but was stripped of the football by Jeremiah Castille, who then fell on the ball at the three-yard line. Denver deliberately took a safety and handed the Browns another heartbreaking defeat one step from the Super Bowl, 38-33.

Kosar was 26-of-41 for 356 yards with the three touchdowns and an interception; he was sacked twice. Byner rushed the ball 15 times for 67 yards with the touchdown and had seven receptions for 120 yards with the touchdown. Mack carried the ball 12 times for 61 yards. Elway was 14-of-26 for 281 yards with the three touchdowns and a pick and was sacked twice. Winder had 20 rushes for 72 yards and three catches for 34 yards with the touchdown. Jackson had four receptions for 134 yards with the touchdown, and Nattiel caught five balls for 95 yards with the touchdown.

Two years later, on January 14, 1990, also in Denver, the Browns and Broncos met again for the AFC title. Unfortunately for the Browns, the third time was not the charm. In fact, they were held scoreless for the entire first half while Denver scored 10 points on the strength of a 29-yard field goal by David Treadwell and a 70-yard touchdown pass from Elway to Mike Young. The Browns made it 10-7 when Kosar hit Brennan on a 27-yard touchdown pass in the third quarter. A five-yard touchdown pass from Elway to Orson Mobley and a seven-yard touchdown run by Winder upped the Broncos lead to 24-7. But, just like the game two years earlier, the Browns wouldn't die. They cut the deficit to 24-21 entering the fourth quarter on a 10-yard scoring strike from Kosar to Brennan and a short touchdown run by Tim Manoa. This time, though, there would be no heartbreaking ending. Elway hit Winder on a 39-yard touchdown pass, and Treadwell shut the door on Cleveland with 34- and 31-yard field goals, as the Broncos won 37-21.

Kosar, battling arm problems he had been dealing with throughout the season, was 19-of-44 for 210 yards with the two touchdowns and three interceptions; he was sacked four times. Mack carried the ball six times for 36 yards. Langhorne had five receptions for 78 yards, and Brennan had five catches for 58 yards. Elway was 20-of-36 for 385 yards with the three touchdowns and was sacked once. He ran the ball five times for 39 yards, including a 25-yarder. Young had two receptions for 123 yards with the touchdown, and Vance Johnson caught seven balls for 91 yards.

24. Bill Nelsen. Nelsen was a Cleveland quarterback from 1968-72. He was traded from Pittsburgh on May 14, 1968, when Frank Ryan began having arm troubles. Despite knee problems,

Nelsen in 1968 completed 152 of 293 passes for 2,366 yards with 19 touchdowns and 10 interceptions. He started in place of the struggling Ryan on October 5 against the Steelers and led the Browns to a 31-24 triumph over his former club. The next week he nearly engineered a comeback win in losing a close one to the Cardinals. Then, beginning with a 30-20 upset of the Colts in Baltimore on October 20, the Browns won eight straight games, scoring 30 or more points in the first seven. In a three-week stretch from November 17 to December 1, they hung up 45, 47, and 45 points, respectively. Nelsen connected with Milt Morin on an 87-yard pass play against the Eagles on November 24 for his longest completion as a Brown.

The Browns wound up 10-4 and Century Division champions. They upset Dallas in the playoffs but were flattened by Baltimore in the NFL Championship game. The next year Nelsen led the team to a 10-3-1 record and another Century Division title. Included was an 18-of-25, 255-yard, five-touchdown performance in a 42-10 bashing of the Cowboys and a 290-yard, two-touchdown performance in a 28-24 triumph over the Bears at Wrigley Field. He also hooked up with Paul Warfield on an 82-yard touchdown pass in a 27-21 victory over the Cardinals in St. Louis on December 14. Behind Nelsen's 18-of-27, 219-yard, one-touchdown performance, the Browns routed the Cowboys again 38-14 in the Eastern Conference title game at the Cotton Bowl. A week later he was picked off twice as the visiting Browns were manhandled by the Vikings 27-7 in the NFL title game. He was a Pro Bowler that season.

In 1970 Nelsen completed 159 of 313 passes for 2,156 yards with 16 touchdowns and 16 interceptions as the Browns went 7-7 and missed the playoffs. The next year he completed 174 of 325 passes for 2,319 yards with 13 touchdowns but also

23 picks as the Browns won the weak Central Division title but lost badly at home to Baltimore in the divisional playoffs. He lost his starting job to Mike Phipps in Week 2 of the 1972 season. A fifth knee operation prompted him to retire after the season. Overall, he completed 689 of 1,314 passes for 9,725 yards with 71 touchdowns and 71 interceptions.

25. William Green. Green was a first-round draft choice in 2002. His rookie season that year was his best, as he rushed for 887 yards and six touchdowns. The majority of his success came in the final seven games when he totaled 726 yards, including 114- and 119-yard performances in wins at New Orleans and Jacksonville, respectively. He also had 16 receptions for 113 yards.

In the season finale against the Falcons at home, with the Browns' playoff hopes hanging in the balance, Green broke free for a memorable 64-yard touchdown run that provided the final points in Cleveland's 24-16 victory. With sold-out Cleveland Browns Stadium in an uproar as Green was running toward the end zone, Browns radio play-by-play man Jim Donovan's "Run, William, Run!" will be ingrained in the minds of those who listened forever.

Despite numerous off-the-field issues, Green also led the Browns in rushing yards in 2003 with 559, including a 115-yard performance in a 33-13 upset of the Steelers and a 145-yard, one-touchdown game in a 13-7 win over Oakland the very next week. He rushed for 585 yards in 2004, including a 115-yard performance in a 34-17 triumph over the Bengals. His injury-plagued 2005 season was his last. He was released right before the start of the 2006 season. Overall, he had 568 rushes for 2,109 yards with nine touchdowns and 45 receptions for 277 yards.

STARTER LEVEL

If you're to come up with the right answers to these 25 questions, you'll have to have some knowledge of Browns history. Have at it!

1. I was a running back who was chosen in the second round of the 1973 draft out of the University of Oklahoma. I spent nine seasons with Cleveland. Who am I? *Answer on page 47.*

2. Which West Coast team did the Browns defeat in the 1950 NFL Championship game? *Answer on page 48.*
   a. Seattle Seahawks
   b. San Francisco 49ers
   c. Los Angeles Rams
   d. San Diego Chargers

3. The Browns and which AFC North rival combined for 106 points, the second most in NFL history, on November 28, 2004? *Answer on page 49.*

4. Which veteran quarterback was traded from Detroit on May 1, 1985, to tutor Bernie Kosar until the rookie was ready to take over the starting duties? *Answer on page 51.*

5. The expansion Browns won their first game on Halloween day in 1999 against the New Orleans Saints in the

Superdome when Tim Couch completed a last-second, 56-yard Hail Mary pass to _____. *Answer on page 52.*
a. Dennis Northcutt
b. Darrin Chiaverini
c. Kevin Johnson
d. Leslie Shepherd

6. Who returned two kickoffs for touchdowns in a 41-34 victory over the Chiefs in Kansas City on December 20, 2009? *Answer on page 53.*

7. The bizarre "Bottlegate" incident on December 16, 2001, in which angry fans threw thousands of plastic bottles from the stands, littering large parts of both end zones, in response to what they believed—and what turned out to be—a terrible officiating call occurred during a 15-10 defeat to what current AFC South team? *Answer on page 55.*

8. Match the seasons on the left with the records on the right. *Answer on page 56.*

1986	10-6
1980	9-6-1
1988	11-5
1989	12-4

9. Which former backup to Peyton Manning in Indianapolis came out of nowhere to lead the Browns to two wins and a remarkable performance in a near-miss playoff loss to Pittsburgh on January 5, 2003? *Answer on page 60.*

10. Match the players on the left with the nicknames on the right. *Answer on page 62.*

Frank Pitts	"Doc"
Eric Turner	"Rocky"
Orlando Brown	"The Jet"
Jim Kanicki	"Bad Moon"
Don Cockroft	"Tonto"
Frank Gatski	"The Train"
Dick Ambrose	"Dopey"
Walter Roberts	"Shaf"
Dick Modzelewski	"The Sheik"
Tony Jones	"The Quiet Storm"
Andre Rison	"Stove Top"
Jerry Sherk	"Little Mo"
Chet Hanulak	"Zeus"
Johnny Brewer	"Donny O"
Bob Kolesar	"Riddler"
Otto Graham	"Big Mo"
Matt Stover	"Smokey"
Ross Fichtner	"E-Rock"
Johnny Davis	"The Assassin"
Marion Motley	"Gunner"
Dick Schafrath	"The Flea"
Don Phelps	"Bam-Bam"
Ed Modzelewski	"Automatic"
Eddie Johnson	"B-1 Bomber"
Courtney Brown	"T-Bone"

11. I have the same name as a now passed-on music icon and spent five solid seasons from 1991-95 as a wide receiver. Who am I? *Answer on page 62.*

12. Match the majority owners on the left with the seasons they owned the Browns on the right. *Answer on page 63.*

Randy Lerner	1999-2002
Art McBride	1961-95
Al Lerner	1953-60
Dave Jones	2002-12
Jimmy Haslam	1946-52
Art Modell	2012-

13. Against which AFC North team did the Browns win the unforgettable "Ricochet" game on November 18, 2007? *Answer on page 66.*

14. Kevin Mack and Earnest Byner had the distinction of being the third running-back duo in NFL history to each rush for 1,000 yards in the same season. True or false? *Answer on page 67.*

15. Match the first-round draft picks on the left with the years they were drafted on the right. *Answer on page 70.*

Kellen Winslow	2007
Kamerion Wimbley	2005
Braylon Edwards	2004
Joe Thomas	2006

16. To which AFC East team did the Browns lose 42-0 in Bud Carson's final game as head coach? *Answer on page 71.*

17. Blanton Collier was Cleveland's head coach from 1963-70. In which three seasons of his tenure did the Browns fail to qualify for the postseason? *Answer on page 72.*

a. 1963, 1966, 1970   b. 1963, 1967, 1970

c. 1963, 1965, 1969   d. 1966, 1968, 1969

18. The Browns and New York Giants finished the 1950 season tied for first place in the American Conference with 10-2 records. The Browns won the December 17 playoff game in Cleveland by what score? *Answer on page 73.*

a. 9-3   b. 9-7

c. 8-3   d. 8-0

19. The Browns defeated the Baltimore Colts 41-23 on November 27, 1983, at home to improve to 8-5 on the season. They wound up qualifying for the playoffs. True or false? *Answer on page 74.*

20. Match the dates on the left with the playoff defeats on the right. *Answer on page 76.*

January 14, 1990	Miami 24, Browns 21
January 17, 1988	Houston 24, Browns 23
December 24, 1988	Denver 37, Browns 21
January 4, 1986	Denver 38, Browns 33

21. Forrest Gregg lost his first 11 games as head coach in 1975. True or false? *Answer on page 80.*

22. How many games did the Browns lose in Three Rivers Stadium before they finally notched win number one there? *Answer on page 81.*

23. I was a wide receiver who graced the cover of the September 8, 1980, edition of *Sports Illustrated*. Who am I? *Answer on page 86.*

24. Which Browns record did Dub Jones break, and which NFL record did he tie, on November 25, 1951, in a home game against the Chicago Bears? *Answer on page 87.*

25. Against which Texas team did Doug Dieken score his only career touchdown? *Answer on page 89.*

STARTER LEVEL – ANSWERS

1. Greg Pruitt. I led the Browns in rushing yards every season from 1974-78. In 1975 I rushed for 1,067 yards with a team-leading eight touchdowns. In 1976 I had exactly 1,000 rushing yards and tied Cleo Miller for the team lead with four touchdowns on the ground. The next year I gained 1,086 yards on the ground, and in 1978 I had 960 rushing yards.

I rushed for a career-high 214 yards on December 14, 1975, at home against the Kansas City Chiefs. I had 191 rushing yards on October 17, 1976, against the Falcons in Atlanta. My longest run from scrimmage was a 78-yarder for a touchdown in a 44-7 romp over Kansas City on October 30, 1977. I had also caught many passes in my career and, due to a season-ending injury I suffered in a 1979 game at St. Louis, later in my career I became less of a runner and even more of a receiver out of the backfield; I had 50 receptions for 444 yards with five touchdowns in 1980 and career

Greg Pruitt tries to elude a Bengals defender, October 13, 1974. (The Cleveland Press Collection, Michael Schwartz Library, Cleveland State University)

highs of 65 catches and 636 receiving yards plus four touchdowns in 1981.

I also led the Browns in punt returns and punt return yards every season from 1973-75, kickoff returns in 1973 and 1975, and kickoff return yards from 1973-74. On October 27, 1974, I returned a punt 72 yards late in the game that led to the winning touchdown in a dramatic home win over Denver. Two weeks later on November 10 at New England I returned a kickoff 88 yards for a touchdown.

I was traded to the Los Angeles Raiders on April 28, 1982. Overall, I rushed the ball 1,158 times for 5,496 yards with 25 touchdowns, and I had 323 receptions for 3,022 yards with 17 touchdowns. I returned 58 kickoffs for 1,523 yards and 56 punts for 659 yards. I had 10,700 career combined net yards, with my high of 1,798 coming in 1975. I was a Pro Bowler from 1973-74 and 1976-77.

2. c. Los Angeles Rams. A week earlier, to reach the NFL title game both teams won tiebreaker playoff games. The host Browns, who were 10-2 in the regular season, defeated the New York Giants 8-3 to win the American Conference, and the host Rams, who were 9-3 in the regular season, beat the Chicago Bears 24-14 to win the National Conference. The Browns-Rams game was a wild one played on Christmas Eve in Cleveland Municipal Stadium. It was a game of big plays, beginning with Bob Waterfield's 82-yard touchdown pass to Glenn Davis to give Los Angeles a 7-0 first-quarter lead. The Browns tied the game on Otto Graham's 27-yard touchdown pass to Dub Jones. Dick Hoerner's three-yard touchdown run gave the Rams a 14-7 lead after one quarter. The Browns cut the deficit to 14-13 at halftime when Graham hit Dante Lavelli on a 37-yard touchdown pass.

Graham and Lavelli hooked up again on a 39-yard scoring strike in the third quarter to give the Browns their first lead at 20-14. Hoerner's one-yard touchdown run put the Rams back on top 21-20. Larry Brink returned a fumble six yards to increase the Los Angeles lead to 28-20 entering the fourth quarter. Cleveland wouldn't quit. Graham hit Rex Bumgardner on a 14-yard touchdown pass to make the score 28-27. Lou Groza's 16-yard field goal with 28 seconds remaining proved to be the winning points in a 30-28 Browns victory.

Graham was 22-of-33 for 298 yards with the four touchdowns and an interception. He also ran the ball 12 times for 99 yards. Lavelli had 11 receptions for 128 yards with the two touchdowns, while Jones caught four balls for 80 yards with the touchdown. Waterfield was 18-of-31 for 312 yards with the touchdown and four picks. Hoerner carried the ball 24 times for 86 yards with the two touchdowns. Tom Fears had nine receptions for 136 yards, including a 44-yarder from Waterfield, while Davis caught two passes for 88 yards with the touchdown.

3. Cincinnati Bengals. The Browns, who entered 3-7, lost to the 4-6 Bengals 58-48 in Paul Brown Stadium. Between the two teams, there were almost 1,000 total yards gained—504 for Cincinnati and 462 for Cleveland.

Kelly Holcomb was 30-of-39 for 413 yards with five touchdowns and two interceptions and was sacked three times. William Green rushed the ball 15 times for 75 yards, including a 46-yarder, with a touchdown. Antonio Bryant had eight receptions for 131 yards with two touchdowns. Dennis Northcutt had five receptions for 87 yards, including a 39-yarder from Holcomb, and Steve Heiden caught seven balls for 82 yards with three touchdowns. Carson Palmer was 22-of-29 for 251 yards with four touchdowns and three picks. Rudi Johnson rushed the ball 26 times for 202 yards, including a 52-yarder, with two touchdowns. Chad Johnson had 10 receptions for 117 yards with a touchdown, and T.J. Houshmandzadeh had four catches for 79 yards with two touchdowns.

It should come as no surprise that it took only 33 seconds for the first points to go on the board, in the form of a seven-yard touchdown pass from Holcomb to Heiden for a 7-0 Browns lead. Two Palmer touchdown passes—for 18 yards to Kelley Washington and for 46 yards to Chad Johnson—put the Bengals up by seven, but a 23-yard field goal by Phil Dawson cut the deficit to 14-10 after the first quarter. Dawson began the second quarter with a 29-yard field goal, but the rest of the quarter belonged to the Bengals in the form of a three-yard touchdown pass from Palmer to Houshmandzadeh and a pair of field goals by Shayne Graham. Cincinnati led 27-13 at the half.

Both teams had just scratched the surface, for in the second half the scoreboard nearly blew a fuse. Holcomb threw three touchdown passes in the third quarter alone—a 20-yarder to Heiden and both a nine-yarder and 55-yarder to Bryant. Also in the third the Bengals scored twice, a 53-yard touchdown pass from Palmer to Houshmandzadeh and a seven-yard touchdown run by Rudi Johnson. The Browns trailed 41-34 heading into the fourth quarter. A 36-yard field goal by Graham made it 44-34, but the Browns scored two touchdowns in 29 seconds—a one-yard run by Green and a one-yard pass from Holcomb to Heiden—to forge ahead 48-44 with 10:22 to go. Some four minutes later, though, the Bengals took back the lead 51-48 when Rudi Johnson scored on a seven-yard run.

They put the icing the cake with 1:43 left when Deltha O'Neal intercepted a Holcomb pass and returned it 31 yards for a touchdown. Butch Davis resigned after the game.

4. Gary Danielson. Danielson went undrafted in 1974 out of Purdue University. He spent 1974 and 1975 in the World Football League before signing with the Lions in 1976. He got virtually no playing time that season and then some in 1977. In 1978 he completed 199 of 351 passes for 2,294 yards with 18 touchdowns and 17 interceptions, including a 26-of-33, 352-yard, five-touchdown, one-interception performance in a Week 15 45-14 rout of the Minnesota Vikings.

Two years later, in 1980, Danielson nearly led the Lions to their first playoff berth in a decade when he completed 244 of 417 passes for a career-high 3,223 yards with 13 touchdowns and 11 interceptions. He went 23-of-36 for 348 yards with three touchdowns and a pick in a Week 5 loss at Atlanta, and in a Week 15 win over Tampa Bay he was 29-of-44 for 360 yards with a touchdown. After seeing little action in 1981, in the strike-shortened 1982 season he completed 100 of 197 passes for 1,343 yards with 10 touchdowns and 14 interceptions as Detroit qualified for the expanded postseason with a 4-5 record, but he saw no playing time in the Lions' first-round loss to the Redskins in Washington.

In 1983 Danielson saw limited action during a 9-7 regular season that brought an NFC Central Division title, but he went the entire way in a heartbreaking 24-23 divisional playoff loss to the 49ers in San Francisco, a game in which he was 24-of-38 for 236 yards but also threw five interceptions. In his last season as a Lion, 1984, he completed 252 of 410 passes for 3,076 yards with 17 touchdowns and 15 interceptions.

In Danielson's first year with the Browns, 1985, he directed them to a 2-2 start before suffering a severe right shoulder injury in a Week 5 win at home against New England. He returned to action against the Bengals on November 24 and hooked up with Clarence Weathers for a perfect 72-yard pass play that went for a touchdown, the Browns' only pass of the entire second half, in a key 24-6 victory. The next week against the Giants in the Meadowlands Danielson reinjured his shoulder but was gutsy in leading two late drives that were major factors in a thrilling upset of New York 35-33. The win, his last action of the season, was the impetus for Cleveland's AFC Central Division title.

Danielson was slated to be the starter again in 1986, but he missed the entire season after fracturing his left ankle in the final preseason game on August 28 against the Raiders in Los Angeles. He spent two more years with the Browns in which he saw little action to end his career. Overall with the Browns, he completed 153 of 248 passes for 1,879 yards with 12 touchdowns and seven interceptions.

5. c. Kevin Johnson. The Browns, who came in 0-7, trailed 16-14 when Couch let it fly and the rookie Johnson came down with the ball on the right side of the Saints' end zone. It was Johnson's second touchdown reception of the day; his 24-yard catch from Couch in the third quarter had given the Browns a 14-10 lead. He had four receptions for 96 yards.

The Saints took a 7-0 first-quarter lead when Billy Joe Hobert threw a five-yard touchdown pass to Keith Poole. The Browns tied the score midway through the second quarter on a 27-yard touchdown pass from Couch to Marc Edwards. Doug Brien's 49-yard field goal with eight seconds left in the second quarter put New Orleans on top by three at halftime. About seven-and-a-half minutes after the Browns took their 14-10 lead, Brien booted a 22-yard field goal to pull the Saints within 14-13 heading into the fourth quarter. Brien's 46-yarder with only 21 seconds to go seemingly gave the Saints a 16-14 victory—that is until Couch and Johnson's dramatic game winner at the end.

Couch was 11-of-19 for 193 yards with the three touchdowns and was sacked twice. Tolliver was 9-of-20 for 92 yards with an interception. Ricky Williams, who many Browns fans wanted the team to draft instead of Couch with the number-one pick in the 1999 draft, rushed the ball 40 times for 179 yards.

As for Johnson, a second-round draft pick in 1999 from Syracuse University, he led all NFL rookies that year—and the Browns, too—with 66 receptions, 986 receiving yards, and eight touchdown catches. He set team rookie records for receptions and receiving yards. In 2000 he was the Browns leader in receptions and receiving yards. The next year he led the team with 84 receptions, 1,097 receiving yards, and nine touchdown catches. He had an eight-catch, 153-yard, one-touchdown performance in a loss at Cincinnati on October 14 and a six-catch, 113-yard, one-touchdown performance in a home win over the same Bengals on November 25. In 2002 he led Cleveland in receptions. His best game was a four-reception, 140-yard performance in a playoff loss at Pittsburgh. He was released after nine games in 2003. Overall, he had 315 receptions for 3,836 yards with 23 touchdowns.

6. Josh Cribbs. Cribbs's first touchdown return went for 100 yards late in the first quarter and gave the Browns a 10-3 lead. Kansas City forged ahead 24-13 with three straight

Josh Cribbs returns a kickoff 103 yards for a touchdown, his second kickoff return touchdown on the day, in a 41-34 win over the Chiefs, December 20, 2009. (AndersonsClevelandDesign.com)

second-quarter touchdowns, the last of which was a 21-yard fumble return by Andy Studebaker with 2:44 to go. Cribbs's second touchdown return came on the ensuing kickoff and went for 103 yards to pull the Browns within 24-20 at the half. Jerome Harrison ran for a 71-yard touchdown in the third quarter and for eight- and 28-yard touchdowns, respectively, in the fourth period, the last of which was the winning score.

Brady Quinn was 10-of-17 for 66 yards with two interceptions. Harrison had 34 rushes for a team-record 286 yards with the three touchdowns. Cribbs wound up with 269 kickoff return yards on six returns. Matt Cassel was 22-of-40 for 331 yards with two touchdowns and was sacked once. Jamaal Charles ran the ball 25 times for 154 yards, including a 47-yarder for a touchdown from Cassel. Chris Chambers caught five passes for 114 yards, including a 39-yarder from Cassel, with a touchdown.

Cribbs actually had been a quarterback in college for Kent State University. He was signed as an undrafted free agent on April 29, 2005. He led the Browns in kickoff returns and kickoff return yards every season he was with the team from 2005-12 and in punt returns and punt return yards from 2007-12. His 1,809 kickoff return yards in 2007 are a team record. He returned eight kickoffs—an NFL record that has since been tied—and three punts for touchdowns. Overall, he had 387 kickoff returns for 10,015 yards and 195 punt returns for 2,154 yards.

Cribbs also played wide receiver. His best year was 2011 when he had 41 receptions for 518 yards with four touchdowns. He was a Pro Bowler in 2007, 2009, and 2012. Cribbs was released on March 12, 2013.

7. Jacksonville Jaguars. The Browns, trailing by five and still in playoff contention, had the ball deep in Jaguars territory late in the game. Tim Couch passed the ball to rookie Quincy Morgan, who was hit by safety James Boyd and struggled to hold onto the ball. After making an apparent catch, Morgan lost the ball temporarily when he hit the ground but recovered his own fumble, which would have made it a catch and given the Browns a first down. That would have allowed them time for four tries to get into the end zone. Couch quickly spiked the ball to stop the clock, which, by rule, ends the option for an instant replay challenge. Referee Terry McAulay, though, ruled the replay buzzer on his belt went off prior to the snap.

Jacksonville's request for a review was honored, and the ruling of a completion was overturned, provoking the bottle-throwing escapade. Due to the danger of this, McAulay ruled the game over and ordered both teams to their respective locker rooms with 48 seconds still left on the clock. Nearly thirty minutes later, however, both sides returned to the field for one last snap to officially complete the game via orders from NFL commissioner Paul Tagliabue.

Couch was 21-of-30 for 184 yards, including a 44-yard strike to JaJuan Dawson, with an interception and was sacked three times. Mark Brunell was 20-of-35 for 202 yards with a touchdown and two picks, one of which was returned 97 yards for a touchdown by Anthony Henry. Brunell was sacked eight times. Stacey Mack ran the ball 28 times for 115 yards and had three catches for 24 yards. Ex-Brown Keenan McCardell had seven receptions for 61 yards.

8. The 1986 Browns finished 12-4, the 1980 Browns went 11-5, the 1988 Browns were 10-6, and the 1989 Browns finished 9-6-1.

Whereas the focus the year before was the running game, Earnest Byner's early-season injury and the presence of new offensive coordinator Lindy Infante in 1986 led to the unfolding of one of the NFL's premier passing attacks. Despite the tragic death of Don Rogers to a drug overdose some three and a half weeks before training camp began, the Browns rallied to an unbeaten preseason and hung tough in a season-opening 41-31 loss to the defending Super Bowl Champion Bears at Soldier Field. The Browns won four of their next five games, including a rather satisfying 27-24 triumph over the Steelers on October 5 in Pittsburgh, highlighted by Gerald "The Ice Cube" McNeil's 100-yard kickoff return for a touchdown just before halftime. The victory was the Browns' first ever in Three Rivers Stadium in 17 tries, finally ending the "Three Rivers Jinx."

Next came an embarrassing home loss to the previously winless Packers, but two dome wins—a come-from-behind job over the Vikings and a 24-9 victory over the Colts—got the Browns back on track. A week later on *Monday Night Football* Bernie Kosar passed for more than 400 yards in outdueling Dan Marino and the visiting Dolphins. After a sound beating by the Raiders in Los Angeles, the Browns rebounded to improve to 8-4 with a 37-31 sudden-death win at home against the Steelers when Kosar hit rookie Webster Slaughter for a 36-yard touchdown pass 6:37 into the extra period. The Browns won their last five games, clinching the division title on December 14 by blowing out the supposedly superior Bengals 34-3 at Cincinnati. In the divisional playoffs they came back from 10 points down late in the game to defeat the visiting New York Jets 23-20 in double overtime. In the AFC Championship, also at home, Kosar found Brian Brennan on a spectacular 48-yard touchdown catch-and-run late in the game that gave Cleveland a 20-13 lead and an apparent berth in Super Bowl XXI. But John Elway's infamous "Drive" was the impetus for Denver's stunning 23-20 overtime win.

The 1980 team was the second edition of the Kardiac Kids squad of 1979. If the 1979 Browns had made a habit of late-game heroics, the 1980 team turned it into an art form. After starting the season 0-2, the team won 10 of 12, including consecutive close calls over Green Bay (26-21), Pittsburgh (27-26), Chicago (27-21), and Baltimore (28-27). Included also was a memorable 17-14 upset of Houston on November 30 at the Astrodome in a battle of two 8-4 teams for the top spot in the AFC Central Division. Clarence Scott's late interception of Ken Stabler iced the victory that not only gave the Browns sole possession of first place for the first time in three years but also caused an estimated 15,000 fans to show up at Hopkins Airport, causing thousands of dollars' damage, upon the team's near midnight arrival that evening.

The Browns had a chance to nail down a playoff berth with a win at Minnesota in Week 15. The Vikings, though, gave the Kardiac Kids a taste of their own medicine. The Browns squandered a 14-point fourth-quarter lead but were still in good shape, leading by one with just four seconds to go and Minnesota 46 yards from the Cleveland end zone. Tommy Kramer heaved one down the right sideline into a sea of purple and orange. The ball was batted by Thom Darden, and as fate would have it, fell into the left hand of Ahmad Rashad as the Vikings' receiver backpedaled—cradling the ball against his body—into the end zone. Rashad's miracle catch not only gave the Vikings a stunning 28-23 victory but also the NFC Central Division title. It also turned the Browns' season finale seven days later in Cincinnati into a must-win (or tie) unless wild-card rival New England, which owned the head-to-head tiebreaker over Cleveland, could manage to lose to the 1-14 Saints (they didn't). The Browns held off a late charge by the Bengals in a wild 27-24 triumph that gave the franchise its first division title in nine years. Two weeks later the Browns lost a divisional playoff 14-12 at home to the Oakland Raiders in the infamous Red Right 88 game.

The 1988 Browns were many prognosticators' preseason picks to represent the AFC in the Super Bowl when an avalanche of quarterback injuries that began when Kosar was blindsided by Lloyd Burruss in an opening-day win at Kansas City stacked the deck against the team from the start. But with Kosar, Gary Danielson, Mike Pagel, and Don Strock calling the signals at one time or another, the Browns were still able to sneak into the playoffs as a wild card. They qualified when, in the finale, the old pro Strock engineered an unforgettable 28-23 comeback victory over Houston in the snow after his team trailed 23-7. That earned the Browns a matchup with none other than the Oilers in the AFC Wild Card game six days later on Christmas Eve, again in Cleveland. Houston won the penalty-marred contest 24-23.

The 1989 Browns opened the season with two wins, a 51-0 destruction of the Steelers in Pittsburgh and a 38-24 shootout over the Jets at home. The Browns scored just 47 points over the next four games. The lone triumph in the horrific stretch was a 16-13 home win over Denver on Matt Bahr's last-second, 48-yard field goal, the Browns' first win over the Broncos in 15 years. The offense rose from the dead on October 23 against the Bears on *Monday Night Football* as Kosar hooked up with Slaughter for a 97-yard touchdown pass. The 27-7 victory sparked a four-game winning streak that landed the Browns in first place in the AFC Central and gave them a 7-3 record. A 10-10 tie with Kansas City and three straight losses, however, dropped them to 7-6-1 and the brink of playoff elimination.

An overtime win at home against the Vikings—on a Pagel-to-Van Waiters pass on a fake field goal—put the Browns right back in contention, though, and set up a season-ending, Saturday night showdown in Houston for the division title. They jumped out to a big lead, fell behind (with the help of a curious botched lateral attempt by Clay Matthews), then rode the shoulders of Kevin Mack on a late drive to number 34's winning score—a four-yard run with 39 seconds left—and their fourth division title in five years.

After pulling one out of the hat by barely beating Buffalo in a divisional playoff shootout at home—finalized when

Matthews, redeeming himself for his blunder in the Astrodome two weeks earlier, picked off Jim Kelly at the Cleveland one with three seconds to go—the Browns headed for Denver and their third conference title tilt with the Broncos in four years. They fell behind in the madness of Mile High Stadium, cut the margin to three, then watched helplessly as Elway took control in the late going. Denver denied the Browns a trip to the Super Bowl again, this time 37-21.

9. Kelly Holcomb. After backing up Manning in the late 1990s, Holcomb signed as a free agent in the 2000 off-season. He backed up Tim Couch in 2001 and started the first two games in 2002 after Couch was injured during the preseason. He put up impressive numbers against the Chiefs and Bengals—a combined 44-of-69 for 524 yards with five touchdown passes. He replaced an injured Couch again in the season finale and helped the Browns to a win over the visiting Atlanta Falcons that, in the end, put them in the playoffs.

The Browns' opponents in the wild card round were the Steelers in Heinz Field. A 1-yard touchdown run by William Green gave Cleveland a 7-0 lead just 1:16 into the game. Twenty-two seconds into the second quarter the Browns upped their lead to 14-0 on a 32-yard touchdown pass from Holcomb to Dennis Northcutt. Some five minutes later Antwaan Randle El returned a Chris Gardocki punt 66 yards for a touchdown to cut the Browns' lead to 14-7. Phil Dawson kicked a 31-yard field goal with 49 seconds left in the second quarter to put the Browns up 17-7 at halftime.

The Browns extended their lead to 27-14 early in the fourth quarter, but the Steelers cut it to 27-21 on a three-yard touchdown pass from Tommy Maddox to Jerame Tuman with

12:28 to go. Some two minutes later, though, Holcomb connected with Andre' Davis for a 22-yard touchdown pass to increase Cleveland's lead to 33-21. The Steelers wouldn't be denied, however. They trimmed their deficit to 33-28 with 3:06 left when Maddox hit Hines Ward on a 5-yard touchdown pass. They took their first—and only—lead with 54 seconds remaining on a three-yard touchdown run by Chris Fuamatu-Ma'afala. The final score was 36-33.

Holcomb was 26-of-43 for 429 yards with three touchdowns and an interception. His yardage total is the eighth most in a postseason game in NFL history. Kevin Johnson had four receptions for 140 yards, including an 83-yarder from Holcomb. Northcutt caught six balls for 92 yards with two touchdowns. Maddox was 30-of-48 for 367 yards with three touchdowns and two picks. Amos Zereoue rushed the ball 13 times for 73 yards, including a 36-yarder. Ward had 11 receptions for 104 yards with the touchdown. Plaxico Burress had six receptions for 100 yards with a touchdown, and Randle El caught five balls for 85 yards.

Holcomb beat out Couch for the starting job in 2003, but he simply was not consistent enough to hold on to it. He and Couch each started eight games, and neither could really get much going during a 5-11 season. Holcomb did have his moments, though, one being a 29-of-35, 392-yard, three-touchdown day in a 44-6 rout of the Arizona Cardinals on November 16, 2003. A year later, on November 28, 2004, he was 30-of-39 for 413 yards with five touchdowns and two interceptions in a 58-48 defeat at Cincinnati. The 2004 season was Holcomb's last in Cleveland. Overall, he completed 323 of 507 passes for 3,438 yards with 26 touchdowns and 21 interceptions.

10.

Frank Pitts	"Riddler"
Eric Turner	"E-Rock"
Orlando Brown	"Zeus"
Jim Kanicki	"Smokey"
Don Cockroft	"Donny O"
Frank Gatski	"Gunner"
Dick Ambrose	"Bam-Bam"
Walter Roberts	"The Flea"
Dick Modzelewski	"Little Mo"
Tony Jones	"T-Bone"
Andre Rison	"Bad Moon"
Jerry Sherk	"The Sheik"
Chet Hanulak	"The Jet"
Johnny Brewer	"Tonto"
Bob Kolesar	"Doc"
Otto Graham	"Automatic"
Matt Stover	"Stove Top"
Ross Fichtner	"Rocky"
Johnny Davis	"B-1 Bomber"
Marion Motley	"The Train"
Dick Schafrath	"Shaf"
Don Phelps	"Dopey"
Ed Modzelewski	"Big Mo"
Eddie Johnson	"The Assassin"
Courtney Brown	"The Quiet Storm"

11. Michael Jackson. I was a sixth-round draft choice in 1991 from the University of Southern Mississippi. In my rookie season that year I had 17 receptions for 268 yards with two touchdowns; included was a three-catch, 82-yard game in a

20-0 win at New England on September 8 in which I was on the receiving end of a fourth-quarter, 65-yard touchdown pass from Bernie Kosar, my first touchdown as a pro. The next season I had 47 receptions for both a team-leading 755 yards and seven touchdowns. I had a five-reception, 98-yard, one-touchdown game on a Monday night against Miami and a six-catch, 96-yard, one-touchdown game at Cincinnati.

In 1993 I led the Browns with both 756 receiving yards and eight touchdown receptions. I caught five balls for 105 yards with a 30-yard touchdown catch from Kosar that turned out to be the winning score in a 23-13 Monday night upset of the 49ers on September 13 in Cleveland. I had two receptions for 106 yards with a 62-yard touchdown catch from Vinny Testaverde that gave us a 7-0 second-quarter lead en route to a crucial 28-23 victory over visiting Pittsburgh on October 24. The next year we finished 11-5 and qualified for the playoffs. I had both a team-leading seven receptions and 122 receiving yards in our 20-13 win over visiting New England in an AFC Wild Card game.

In 1995 I caught 44 balls for both a team-leading 714 yards and nine touchdowns. Included was a seven-reception, 157-yard performance, including 70- and 30-yard touchdown catches, respectively, from Testaverde in a season-opening defeat at New England. On November 19 against Green Bay I caught five passes for 83 yards with two touchdowns. When the Browns relocated to Baltimore the next year, I went right along with them. Overall, I had 170 receptions for 2,797 yards with 28 touchdowns in my Browns career.

12. Randy Lerner was the majority owner from 2002-12. Art McBride was the team's majority owner from 1946-52. Al

Lerner was the majority owner from 1999-2002. Dave Jones was the majority owner from 1953-60. Jimmy Haslam has been the majority owner since 2012. Art Modell was the majority owner from 1961-95.

Randy Lerner took over for his father Al as majority owner when the latter passed away seven games into the 2002 season. The Browns finished 9-7 and qualified for the playoffs. It was downhill from there as Lerner's Browns won six or fewer games in eight of the next nine seasons. He was majority owner through October 25, 2012.

McBride was responsible for bringing the Browns to Cleveland. It was ironic, too, because he was never interested in football—that is until he paid a visit to South Bend, Indiana, one day in October 1940. A wealthy businessman in his fifties known to almost everyone in Cleveland as "Mickey," McBride journeyed to South Bend to watch the hometown Fighting Irish of the University of Notre Dame—where his son Arthur, Jr., had recently enrolled—defeat a helpless opponent. He enjoyed the Notre Dame game so much, he began to follow the fortunes of the Fighting Irish religiously and gained an interest in professional football as well. Little did he know, however, that his presence at that Notre Dame game would be the impetus for nearly seventy years of pro football in a town just more than 250 miles eastward. About two years after witnessing that Notre Dame game, McBride made a failed attempt at purchasing the fledgling Cleveland Rams franchise of the NFL. However, on September 3, 1944, he was awarded a Cleveland franchise in the new All-America Football Conference.

The man McBride hired as head coach was Ohio legend Paul Brown, who had compiled a prolific record as head coach at Massillon Washington High School, as well as Ohio State

University and the Great Lakes Naval Training Center outside of Chicago. McBride's Browns (named after the coach himself) won all four AAFC championships, compiling an almost surreal overall record, including postseason, of 52-4-3. His 1950 team joined the NFL and won the championship, defeating the Los Angeles Rams 30-28. His 1951 and 1952 clubs played for championships but lost to the Rams and Lions, respectively.

Al Lerner, a successful businessman, saw his "new era" expansion Browns win just five of 32 games combined from 1999-2000. The team improved to 7-9 in 2001 and was 3-4 the next year when he passed away on October 23, 2002.

Jones, a businessman and former Cleveland Indians director, saw his 1953 Browns lose to Detroit in the NFL title game, but his 1954 and 1955 teams rebounded by winning back-to-back championships, crushing both the Lions and Rams, respectively. After dropping to 5-7 without a retired Otto Graham in 1956, the Browns, with rookie Jim Brown, returned to the title game in 1957 but were pounded by the Lions. The 1958 Browns tied the Giants for first place at 9-3 in the Eastern Conference but lost to them 10-0 in a playoff. Both the 1959 and 1960 Browns had winning records but failed to win their conference.

Truck stop business magnate, and former minority owner of the Pittsburgh Steelers, Haslam took over as majority owner on October 25, 2012, with the team's record at 1-6. They would finish 5-11. Other than one season, the Browns under Haslam have gotten worse every year, bottoming out at 1-15 in 2016.

Modell had a background in the advertising business in New York City. His first two teams finished 8-5-1 and 7-6-1, respectively, and out of the postseason. He fired Paul Brown after the 1962 season. With assistant coach Blanton

Collier replacing Brown, Modell's 1963 team finished 10-4 and one game behind the Giants. The 1964 Browns upset the Baltimore Colts 27-0 for the NFL championship. The Browns returned to the title game three more times before the 1960s were through but lost them all. They had three losing years in the 1970s and qualified for the postseason only twice. Heartbreaking playoff defeats took center stage in the 1980s, with Red Right 88, a blown 18-point lead at Miami, The Drive, and The Fumble. The Browns had just one winning season in Modell's last six seasons as owner. He did the unthinkable in 1996 by relocating the team to Baltimore, where it would become the Ravens.

13. Baltimore Ravens. There have been countless Browns games throughout the years that have provided crazy plays and wacky ways. But what occurred at the end of regulation in this game at M&T Bank Stadium might just take the cake. The Browns, just off a heartbreaking defeat at Pittsburgh and a thrilling triumph over the Seahawks prior to that, were in the midst of their third straight game that would go down to the wire. At 5-4, they were desperate for a win to keep playoff hopes from becoming little more than a pipe dream.

The Browns, suddenly an offensive juggernaut since Derek Anderson replaced the departed Charlie Frye following an embarrassing home loss to the Steelers in the season opener, seemed to have the game well in hand. They carried a 27-14 lead into the fourth quarter. The 4-5 Ravens, their playoff hopes in even bigger jeopardy than their visitors, refused to die. Three Matt Stover field goals and a 27-yard scoring strike from Kyle Boller to Devard Darling had Baltimore in the lead 30-27 with just 26 seconds to go.

A 39-yard kickoff return by Josh Cribbs gave the Browns the ball on their own 43-yard line. Completions from Anderson to Joe Jurevicius and Braylon Edwards put the ball on the Ravens' 34 with but three seconds remaining. Phil Dawson, who had come up just short on a 52-yard field goal try that would have forced overtime against the Steelers the week before, came on to attempt a 51-yarder. Dawson's boot had more than enough distance this time. However, the ball deflected off of the left upright and, incredibly, onto the top of the support beam beyond the crossbar, then ricocheted back in front of the bar before falling to the ground. It was an extraordinary sequence no observer had ever seen before. The initial ruling was that Dawson's kick was no good. The two officials beneath the goalpost saw only that the ball sprung backwards and tumbled down short of the crossbar.

Players from both sides were undressing in their respective locker rooms, thinking the game was over and that the teams were now tied for second place in the AFC North with 5-5 records when shocking news arrived—the game was not over. Although field goals, by rule, are not reviewable via instant replay, officials had huddled and reversed their original call—the correct decision—making Dawson's three-pointer good, thus knotting the score at 30 and forcing overtime.

The players put their uniforms back on and returned to the field to play the overtime session. Dawson's 33-yard—and somewhat anticlimactic—field goal 5:47 into the extra period gave the Browns an exhilarating 33-30 triumph, sending 71,055 fans home shocked, shaking their heads in disbelief.

14. True. Mack, a rookie, and Byner, in his second season, accomplished the feat in 1985. The first duo to achieve the deed was Miami's Larry Csonka and Mercury Morris in 1972. The second pair to do it was Pittsburgh's Franco Harris and Rocky Bleier in 1976. Mack, a first-round supplemental draft pick in 1984 from Clemson University who spent a year in the USFL, rushed for a team-high 1,104 yards with seven touchdowns on 222 carries. He also had 29 receptions for 297 yards with three touchdowns. Byner, a 10th-round draft choice in 1984 out of East Carolina University, rushed for 1,002 yards with a team-best eight touchdowns on a team-leading 244 carries. He also had 45 catches for 460 yards with two touchdowns.

Mack had three games in which he rushed for 100 yards. The first was on September 29 when he had 130 yards on 16 carries, including a 61-yarder, with a touchdown run in a 21-7 victory over the Chargers at San Diego. The second came the very next week when he gained 115 yards on 20 carries, including a 10-yard touchdown run in the fourth quarter that was the winning points in a 24-20 home win over New England. The last was on November 24 when he ran for 117 yards on 14 carries, including touchdown runs of two and 35 yards in a 24-6 triumph over the visiting Bengals.

Byner twice ran for 100 yards. The first was on November 17 when he gained 109 yards on 15 rushes, including a four-yard touchdown run in the third quarter that were the winning points in a 17-7 win over Buffalo at home. The other came in the season finale on December 22 when he rushed for 101 yards on 15 carries in a loss to the Jets in New York. Three weeks earlier in the same stadium, in a stirring 35-33 victory over the Giants, he had two rushing touchdowns—a two-yarder in the second quarter and a nine-yarder late in the game that was the winning score. In a divisional playoff defeat at Miami he set a Browns postseason record with 161 rushing yards, including 21- and 66-yard touchdown runs.

In the 1989 season finale at Houston in a battle for the AFC Central Division title Mack carried the load on a late drive to his own winning score—a four-yard run with 39 seconds to go—in the Browns' thrilling 24-20 victory. Mack led the Browns in rushing yards from 1986-87 and 1990-92. He led the team in rushing touchdowns in 1986 and from 1990-92. His final year with the Browns was 1993. Overall, he rushed the ball 1,291 times for 5,123 yards with 46 touchdowns and had 197 receptions for 1,602 yards with eight touchdowns. He was a Pro Bowler in 1985 and 1987.

In the 1984 season finale Byner, a rookie, rushed for 188 yards on 21 carries, including two touchdown runs, in a victory over the Oilers at the Astrodome. Earlier that year, in a Week 10 win at Buffalo, he recovered a fumble and raced 55 yards for a touchdown. Also that year, he led the Browns in kickoff returns and kickoff return yards. He had quite a postseason in 1987. In a divisional playoff win over the Colts he had 122 rushing yards with a touchdown plus 36 receiving yards with a touchdown. In an AFC title game loss to the Broncos he had 120 receiving yards with a touchdown plus 67 rushing yards with a touchdown. Unfortunately, he will be remembered by many for his untimely fumble near the goal line toward the end in the Denver game.

Byner was tops on the Browns in rushing yards in 1988. He led the team in rushing touchdowns in 1987 and tied for the team lead in 1988. He also led the club in receptions from 1987-88. Byner was traded to Washington on draft day in 1989 but re-signed as a free agent on May 5, 1994. He tied for the team lead in rushing touchdowns in 1995 and led the team in receptions that year. When the Browns moved to Baltimore in 1996 and became the Ravens, he went right along with them. Overall, he had 862 rushes for 3,364 yards with 27 touchdowns. He had 276 receptions for 2,630 yards with 10 touchdowns.

15. Kellen Winslow was drafted with the sixth overall pick in 2004 out of the University of Miami. Kamerion Wimbley was drafted 13th overall in 2006 out of Florida State University. Braylon Edwards was chosen with the third overall selection from the University of Michigan in 2005. Joe Thomas was the third overall selection in 2007 out of the University of Wisconsin.

Winslow, a tight end, missed most of his rookie season of 2004 because of a Week 2 leg injury. He missed the entire 2005 season due to another leg injury from an off-season motorcycle accident. He recovered nicely, though, for in 2006 he had a team-leading 89 receptions, tied for the most in team history, for 875 yards and three touchdowns. The next season, his only Pro Bowl year, he caught a team-leading 82 balls for 1,106 yards and five touchdowns. This included home wins over Cincinnati, Seattle, and Houston in which, respectively, he had six receptions for 100 yards with a touchdown, 11 receptions for 125 yards, and 10 catches for 107 yards with a touchdown. He tied for the team lead in touchdown receptions in 2008. He was traded to Tampa Bay on February 27, 2009. Overall, he had 219 receptions for 2,459 yards with 11 touchdowns.

A linebacker, Wimbley led the Browns with both 11 sacks and three fumble recoveries in 2006. He had 44 tackles. In 2007 he was the team leader with both five sacks and three forced fumbles. He also had 39 tackles and a pass defended. The next season he had 52 tackles, four sacks, an interception, two passes defended, and a forced fumble. In 2009 he was tops on the Browns with

70

6.5 sacks. He also had 48 tackles, a forced fumble, and a pass defended. He was traded to the Raiders on March 15, 2010. Overall, he had 26.5 sacks, 183 tackles, three fumble recoveries, an interception, six forced fumbles, and four passes defended.

Edwards, a wide receiver, caught an 80-yard touchdown pass from Trent Dilfer in a 26-24 upset of the Packers in Green Bay on September 18, 2005. He had his best—and only Pro Bowl—year in 2007 when he had 80 receptions for both a team-leading 1,289 yards and 16 touchdowns. He had eight receptions for 146 yards with two touchdowns in a 51-45 Week 2 win over the Bengals. He had three touchdown catches in a win over Miami on October 14 and two weeks later caught eight passes for 117 yards with two touchdowns in a win at St. Louis. He led the Browns with both 884 receiving yards in 2006 and 873 receiving yards in 2008. He also led the team with 55 receptions in 2008. He was traded to the New York Jets four games into the 2009 season on October 7. Overall, he had 238 receptions for 3,697 yards with 28 touchdowns.

Thomas, a left offensive tackle, attended Brookfield Central High School in Brookfield, Wisconsin. There, he was ranked as the number 18 offensive tackle prospect in the class of 2003. As a true freshman at the University of Wisconsin, he mainly saw action as a blocking tight end. He was the Badgers' starting left offensive tackle his last three years. As a senior, he won the Outland Trophy as the nation's top interior lineman and was a consensus first-team All-American in helping Wisconsin to a 12-1 record, a school record for wins. He has been a Pro Bowler in each of his 10 seasons with the Browns.

16. Buffalo Bills. The Bills entered the game with a 6-1 record en route to the first of four straight Super Bowl appearances, while the Browns, just off of three AFC title games in four years, came in at just 2-6. With Mike Pagel starting in place of the struggling Bernie Kosar, the Browns got nowhere. It was all Buffalo from the start. Thurman Thomas gave the Bills a 14-0 halftime lead with two touchdown runs—a three-yarder in the first quarter and an 11-yarder in the second. The visitors upped their lead to 21-0 in the third quarter when Jamie Mueller ran it in from a yard out. Thomas scored again in the fourth quarter on an 11-yard touchdown pass from Jim Kelly to make it 28-0. Kenneth Davis scored from three yards out, and Darryl Talley put the icing on the cake with a 60-yard pick-six off of Pagel.

Pagel was 16-of-38 for 195 yards with two interceptions and was sacked once. Brian Brennan had five receptions for 85 yards. Kelly was 14-of-19 for 200 yards with the touchdown and was sacked once. Thomas rushed the ball 17 times for 58 yards with the two touchdowns and had five catches for 65 yards with the touchdown. Andre Reed had seven receptions for 122 yards, including a 43-yarder from Kelly. Carson was fired afterwards.

17. a. 1963, 1966, 1970. Collier, the team's offensive backfield coach in 1962, replaced the fired living legend Paul Brown. Collier's first Browns team reeled off six victories to start the season. They were 9-3 heading into their own personal grave-yard of Tiger Stadium for a December 8 matchup with Detroit. The Browns, who had lost all four games—two of them championship contests—that they had played in the "Motor City," were beaten 38-10, all but ruining their chance to win the Eastern Conference championship. A 27-20 victory in the finale at Washington the next week was meaningless since the Giants beat Pittsburgh the same day, clinching their third consecutive conference crown. New York finished 11-3, one game better than the 10-4 Browns, who missed the postseason for the fifth straight year.

The 1966 Browns lost two of their first three games but recovered to win six of their next seven, including a 30-21 home win over Dallas and a 49-17 rout of the Falcons in Atlanta in games 6 and 7, respectively. The Cowboys got revenge with a 26-14 victory on Thanksgiving. Dallas went on to win the Eastern Conference title with a 10-3-1 record, a game-and-a-half ahead of the 9-5 Browns, who wound up in a second-place tie with Philadelphia.

The Browns, in the first year of the AFL-NFL merger, began the 1970 season with a bang, beating Joe Namath and the New York Jets 31-21 on September 21 in the very first ABC *Monday Night Football* game. It was a night of big plays for the Browns. First, Homer Jones returned the second-half kickoff 94 yards for a touchdown. Billy Andrews put the nail in New York's coffin when he made a diving interception of a Namath pass, got up, and returned it 25 yards for a touchdown with 35 seconds to go.

The Browns were a model of inconsistency but, due to their AFC Central Division rivals' lackluster play as well, stayed in the hunt. They lost out on the division championship on the final day of the season when the Cincinnati Bengals, after a 1-6 start, won their seventh straight game to finish 8-6, a game ahead of the 7-7 Browns, whose victory in Denver later that day, as a result, was meaningless.

18. c. 8-3. The Browns, in their first season in the NFL after having won all four AAFC titles from 1946-49, had lost both regular-season meetings with the Giants—6-0 at home on October 1 and 17-13 on the road on October 22. The winner of the playoff would face the winner of the National Conference playoff contest between the 9-3 Rams and 9-3 Bears that would be played in Los Angeles later that day (a game the Rams wound up winning 24-14).

The only points scored during the first three quarters came on an 11-yard field goal by Lou Groza in the first period. The Giants tied the score at three when Randy Clay booted a 20-yard field goal. Later in the fourth quarter Groza gave the Browns the lead again when he knocked home a 28-yard field goal. The final points were scored when Bill Willis tackled Charlie Conerly in the end zone for a safety. The Browns' middle guard provided another defensive gem when he saved the day late in the game by tackling Gene Roberts from behind at the Browns' four-yard line.

Otto Graham was just 3-of-8 for 43 yards with an interception. He rushed the ball eight times for 70 yards. Dante Lavelli had two receptions for 35 yards. Conerly was 3-of-12 for 48 yards with two picks. Roberts had 12 rushes for 76 yards, including a 32-yarder, and caught a 17-yard pass from Conerly. Eddie Price had 21 carries for 65 yards.

19. False. The Browns barely missed making the playoffs. They were the only one of five 9-7 teams to miss the postseason in 1983. The season started well, as they won four of their first six games, including a 30-24 overtime win at San Diego when Brian Sipe hit Harry Holt on a 48-yard touchdown catch-and-run and a 10-7 triumph over the visiting Jets on a 44-yard field goal by Matt Bahr as time expired.

As the team went into a tailspin—including a six-interception performance by Sipe in a 44-17 defeat at Pittsburgh—Paul McDonald got the starting nod for the October 30 game against Houston. The former USC star did not exactly light up

Cleveland Stadium but did notch a 25-19 overtime win. He faltered the next week as the starter in a loss to Green Bay, a game in which he got yanked in favor of Sipe. With Sipe as the starter again, the Browns won three straight games, including successive shutouts of the Buccaneers and Patriots—the team's first back-to-back bagels in 32 years—and stood at 8-5, just a game behind the 9-4 Steelers in the AFC Central Division with three to go.

The final victory of that three-game winning streak was the drubbing of Baltimore. It was the most points the Browns scored since they hung up 42 against the same Colts more than two years earlier. The Browns were in complete control from the start. They were up 14-3 after one quarter on a short touchdown run by Mike Pruitt and a 15-yard touchdown pass from Sipe to Willis Adams. The two teams traded touchdowns twice in the second quarter—the Browns' scores being a 66-yard touchdown catch-and-run from Sipe to Ozzie Newsome and a 9-yard touchdown pass from Sipe to Dave Logan—as the home team took a 28-17 lead to the locker room. The Browns upped their lead to 38-17 entering the fourth quarter and put it in cruise control the rest of the way.

Sipe was 20-of-33 for 313 yards with the three touchdowns and was sacked once. Pruitt rushed the ball 24 times for 110 yards with two touchdowns. Newsome had eight receptions for 108 yards with the touchdown. Adams caught three balls for 86 yards, including a 58-yarder from Sipe, with the touchdown. Logan had three receptions for 64 yards. Mike Pagel was 15-of-26 for 164 yards with two touchdowns and two picks; he was sacked twice. Randy McMillan ran the ball 11 times for 50 yards with a touchdown and had three receptions for 22 yards with a touchdown. Tracy Porter had four catches for 71 yards.

Aware that a win in Denver on December 4 would forge a first-place tie with Pittsburgh due to the Steelers' upset loss at home to Cincinnati earlier in the day, the Browns ran into a buzz saw—a rookie quarterback by the name of John Elway—who gave Cleveland a Mile High migraine. The former Stanford University star was 16-of-24 for 284 yards with two touchdowns and an interception in a 27-6 rout of the Browns, the first of several Cleveland defeats to Elway-led Denver teams in the years to come.

If the defeat in Denver wasn't bad enough, what followed was. The next week in the Astrodome, an Oilers team that had won just a single game all year long upset the Browns. The 34-27 defeat, a game in which the Browns fought back from a 24-6 deficit to take a late lead, only to lose it, ended any division title hopes and even put their wild card aspirations in jeopardy. A 30-17 victory over Pittsburgh in the season finale at home on December 18 salvaged a winning record and second-place finish; they wound up a game behind the 10-6 Steelers. Seattle's win over New England later that day knocked them out of playoff contention. They lost out to the Seahawks and Broncos, the AFC's two other 9-7 teams, for the two conference wild card berths due to their defeats to both teams during the season.

20. On January 14, 1990, the Browns lost 37-21 to the Broncos at Denver in the AFC Championship game. Two years earlier, on January 17, 1988, they lost 38-33 to the Broncos, also in Denver, in the AFC title game. Later that year, on December 24, they fell 24-23 to Houston in the AFC Wild Card game. On January 4, 1986, they lost to the Dolphins 24-21 at Miami in an AFC Divisional Playoff game.

Although the Browns made it close for a short while, Denver dominated the 1990 Broncos game. The home team was up 10-0 at halftime thanks to a 29-yard field goal by David Treadwell in the first quarter and a 70-yard touchdown pass from John Elway to Mike Young in the second quarter. Brian Brennan caught a 27-yard touchdown pass from Bernie Kosar to make the score 10-7 in the third quarter. Two Broncos touchdowns upped their lead to 24-7 before the Browns pulled within 24-21 entering the fourth quarter on a 10-yard touchdown pass from Kosar to Brennan and a two-yard touchdown run by Tim Manoa. Soon after, Elway hit Sammy Winder on a 39-yard touchdown pass to make it 31-21. Two Treadwell field goals nailed the coffin shut on the Browns.

Kosar was 19-of-44 for 210 yards with the two touchdowns and three interceptions; he was sacked four times. Kevin Mack had six carries for 36 yards. Reggie Langhorne had five receptions for 78 yards, and Brennan caught five balls for 58 yards with the two touchdowns. Elway was 20-of-36 for 385 yards with three touchdowns and was sacked once. He also ran the ball five times for 39 yards, including a 25-yarder. Young had two receptions for 123 yards with the touchdown. Vance Johnson had seven catches for 91 yards.

In the 1988 game against the Broncos the Browns fell behind big time. They trailed 21-3 at halftime and, after an 80-yard catch-and-run touchdown pass from Elway to Mark Jackson, they were down 28-10 early in the third quarter. That's when Kosar and Earnest Byner went to work and led a remarkable comeback that fell just short when, with the visitors down by seven late in the game and the ball on the Broncos' eight-yard line, Byner, bursting off left tackle and smelling the end zone, was stripped of the football by Jeremiah Castille at the three-yard line; Castille then fell on the ball at the three. The play became aptly known as "The Fumble," and Denver, which beat the Browns in "The Drive" game the year before, eked out a second straight trip to the Super Bowl.

Kosar was 26-of-41 for 356 yards with three touchdowns and an interception and was sacked twice. Byner had seven receptions for 120 yards with a touchdown and ran the ball 15 times for 67 yards with a touchdown. Mack had 12 carries for 61 yards and four catches for 28 yards. Elway was 14-of-26 for 281 yards with three touchdowns and an interception and was sacked twice. Winder had 20 rushes for 72 yards and three receptions for 34 yards with a touchdown. Jackson caught four balls for 134 yards with the touchdown, while Ricky Nattiel had five catches for 95 yards with a touchdown.

The loss to Houston was a rematch of the week before when the Browns recovered from a huge deficit to beat the Oilers, also in Cleveland, just to qualify for the postseason. In the playoff game, the Browns fell behind again. Two touchdowns by Allen Pinkett—the first on a 14-yard pass from Warren Moon, the second on a 16-yard run—had the Oilers up 14-3 in the second quarter. Two short field goals by Matt Bahr pulled the Browns within 14-9 at halftime. They forged ahead 16-14 in the third quarter on a 14-yard touchdown pass from Mike Pagel to Webster Slaughter. The fourth quarter, however, belonged to the visitors. Lorenzo White's one-yard touchdown run gave Houston the lead again at 21-16. The lead grew to 24-16 when Tony Zendejas kicked a 49-yard field goal. A short touchdown pass from Pagel to Slaughter with 31 seconds left was too little, too late.

Pagel was 17-of-25 for 179 yards with the two touchdowns and an interception. Byner rushed the ball nine times for 57 yards. Slaughter had five receptions for 58 yards with the two touchdowns, and Langhorne caught six passes for 57 yards. Moon was 16-of-26 for 213 yards with the touchdown and three interceptions, two of them by Felix Wright; he was sacked once. Pinkett had 14 rushes for 82 yards with the touchdown and had two receptions for 24 yards with the touchdown. Drew Hill had five receptions for 73 yards, and Haywood Jeffires had three catches for 52 yards, including a 35-yarder from Moon.

The Browns were heavy underdogs to the Dolphins due to their 8-8 record compared to Miami's 12-4 mark and its high-powered offense led by Dan Marino. After Fuad Reveiz gave the home team a 3-0 first-quarter lead with a 51-yard field goal, the Browns grabbed the attention of the huge Orange Bowl crowd later in the quarter by forging ahead 7-3 on a 16-yard touchdown pass from Kosar to Ozzie Newsome. The guys in orange helmets began to cause some worry to the 75,128 fans in attendance when Byner's hard-fought 21-yard touchdown run in the second quarter gave the Browns a 14-3 halftime lead. The Browns caused some serious heart palpitations among Dolphins fans everywhere, not to mention shocked the football world, by upping their lead to 21-3 in the third quarter when Byner busted loose and raced 66 yards for a touchdown. One of the most stunning upsets in NFL postseason history seemed to be a real possibility. Hanford Dixon and Frank Minnifield were shutting down Miami's "Marks Brothers," wide receivers Mark Duper and Mark Clayton.

The Dolphins, though, would not die. Slowly but surely they cut into their huge deficit. First, Marino hit Nat Moore later in the third quarter on a six-yard touchdown pass. Then Ron Davenport scored on a 31-yard run. The Browns' lead was just 21-17 entering the fourth quarter. Davenport scored again, this time from a yard out, for the winning points. The Browns made a feeble attempt at one last drive, but time ran out.

Kosar was just 10-of-19 for 66 yards with the touchdown and an interception; he was sacked once. Byner rushed the ball 16 times for a Browns postseason record 161 yards with the two touchdowns. As a team, the Browns ran for 251 yards, another team postseason record. Byner also had four receptions for 25 yards. Marino was 25-of-45 for 238 yards with the touchdown and a pick. Davenport had six carries for 48 yards with the two touchdowns. Tony Nathan had 10 receptions for 101 yards, including a 39-yarder from Marino. Bruce Hardy caught five passes for 51 yards.

21. False. Gregg lost his first nine games of the 1975 season. Mike Phipps finally led the Browns to victory on November 23 in an upset of the red-hot Bengals. The team won three of its last five games, but with a poor year from Phipps that was becoming a yearly occurrence—he had four touchdown passes and 19 interceptions—looming large, still wound up 3-11, AFC Central Division cellar dwellers for the second straight year. Nine of the defeats came by 11 points or more.

Phipps, for all intents and purposes, was lost for the season upon getting injured in the 1976 season opener against the New York Jets. Brian Sipe took over and had a rough first few weeks as the starter, but then he led the Browns to eight wins in nine games. They finished 9-5 but behind the division champion Steelers and Bengals, who both finished 10-4.

With Phipps gone—the Browns had traded the much-maligned quarterback and his 81 career interceptions to the

Bears in the off-season—Sipe led the team to a fine start in Gregg's third season of 1977. Cleveland won five of its first seven games, including a 30-27 sudden-death thriller over the Patriots on a Monday night and a 44-7 rout of the Chiefs, and found themselves in an unfamiliar position at the season's halfway mark—in first place looking *down* at Pittsburgh and Cincinnati in the standings. A 10-7 home defeat to the Bengals ignited a horrendous second half of the season in which Sipe was out for the year to a separated left shoulder in a loss to the Steelers. The Browns finished 6-8 and in the division basement. Gregg was fired with one game left, although it was announced publicly as a resignation.

22. Sixteen. The streak began with a 28-9 defeat on November 29, 1970. Prior to moving to brand new Three Rivers that year, the Steelers had spent seven seasons in Pitt Stadium on the University of Pittsburgh campus and 30 prior to that in Forbes Field for the most part.

Not coincidentally, the start of the losing streak coincided with the arrival of Terry Bradshaw in "Steel Town." The young quarterback was Pittsburgh's top pick—and the number one overall selection—in the 1970 NFL Draft, held earlier that year. Although Three Rivers itself was believed by many Browns fans—and even some in the Browns organization—to be "haunted," Bradshaw, the ex-Louisiana Tech University star with a machine gun for a right arm, had much to do with the Steelers' domination of the Browns in Pittsburgh, which came to be known as the "Three Rivers Jinx."

The fact that Pittsburgh was one of the NFL's top teams during much of the streak's duration should make its success against Cleveland at home come as no surprise. However, at the same time they found the going rough in southwestern Pennsylvania, the Browns, average to below average for much of the same time span, were able to muster road wins over other top teams, including Miami in 1970, Oakland in 1973, and both Cincinnati and San Francisco in 1981. One would think that once, just once, they would have pulled one out in Pittsburgh, stolen one, somewhere along the way. At least twice during the streak, officials' calls (questionable, to say the least) in the late stages of games led Browns backers to believe there was something fishy in the air.

Nonetheless, Pittsburgh's mastery of Cleveland at home in this period came during a time when the Browns were on the downswing and the Steelers the upswing. Entering the 1970 season, the Browns had built a rich tradition, having won four NFL Championships—appearing in 11 title games—in their 20 years in the league; they had won eight championships in all, including four in the AAFC. They had treated Pittsburgh like a whipping boy for years, having won 31 of 40 games, including 15 of 20 in Pittsburgh. The Steelers, on the other hand, had never won a title of any kind in their nearly 40-year history except for perhaps that of . . . well . . . loser.

After an easy home win over the Browns in 1971, Pittsburgh's home victory over them in 1972 was notable not for its competitiveness, but for the marking of the changing of the guard. The Browns were an aging team attempting to make one last stand. The Steelers, meanwhile, were in the midst of building a dynasty. Chuck Noll was in his fourth year as head coach and, through excellent drafts, had improved the team from 1-13 his first season to 8-3 entering this December 3 contest against the Browns, who were also 8-3. This battle for

AFC Central supremacy turned into a Three Rivers thrashing as Pittsburgh won in a rout 30-0.

The Steelers went on to win the division title with an 11-3 record. The Browns finished 10-4 and qualified for the playoffs as the AFC wild card team. It would turn out to be the franchise's last postseason appearance until the dawning of the next decade. Both teams were ousted in the playoffs by eventual Super Bowl Champion Miami, the Browns in the divisional round and the Steelers in the conference championship game. With the tide now turned, the Steelers won, with ease, three of the next four home games against the Browns.

Beginning in 1977, the heart of The Jinx took its course, as the next five games in Three Rivers between the "turnpike rivals" hinged on thrilling finishes, suspect officiating calls, and hard hits as usual. In the five games from 1977-81, the Steelers won by just an average of 4.4 points per contest. The following is a recap of the five Browns-Steelers games in Pittsburgh from 1977-81:

*Steelers 35, Browns 31 (November 13, 1977)
-Brian Sipe fractured his left shoulder blade, causing him to miss the rest of the season.
*Steelers 15, Browns 9 (OT) (September 24, 1978)
-In an early-season showdown for first place, Ricky Feacher recovered a fumble on the overtime kickoff deep in Steelers territory. Although television replays confirmed the play was indeed a fumble, officials ruled the play had been blown dead prior to the miscue, and the ball was awarded to Pittsburgh. Minutes later, Bradshaw hit Bennie Cunningham for a 37-yard touchdown pass on a flea flicker.
*Steelers 33, Browns 30 (OT) (November 25, 1979)

Dave Logan celebrates after catching a touchdown pass from Brian Sipe in the Browns' 33-30 overtime loss at Pittsburgh, November 25, 1979. (The Cleveland Press Collection, Michael Schwartz Library, Cleveland State University)

-The Browns entered 8-4, a game behind Pittsburgh and Houston. They squandered leads of 20-6, 27-13, and 30-20. They trailed one time—when Matt Bahr connected on a 37-yard field goal with nine seconds left in sudden death.

*Steelers 16, Browns 13 (November 16, 1980)

-Bradshaw's three-yard touchdown pass to Lynn Swann with 11 seconds to go—a play in which Pittsburgh's wide receiver Theo Bell admitted after the game he'd illegally picked Ron Bolton—gave Pittsburgh the victory and cost the Browns a share of first place.

*Steelers 13, Browns 7 (October 11, 1981)

-Paul McDonald replaced a dazed Sipe, who in the third quarter suffered a concussion on a ferocious hit by Jack Lambert. McDonald led two late drives, but his interception on a tipped pass in the Steelers' end zone killed one; time expired on the other when officials ruled that Reggie Rucker failed to get out of bounds—Rucker claimed he did—after his 17-yard catch moved Cleveland to the Pittsburgh 32-yard line.

The Browns' frustration at their failings in Three Rivers led them to the depths of superstition. They resorted to extreme measures in trying to halt The Jinx. They tried flying to Pittsburgh, they took a bus for a while … they even drove there in cars. They also changed hotels several times.

After lopsided losses at Three Rivers in 1982 and 1983, the Browns were defeated there on last-second field goals the next two years, but the tide was slowly turning back in favor of Cleveland. By the time the 1986 season began, the Browns' talent level was far superior to the Steelers' for the first time since the streak began, and the "Three Rivers Jinx" finally came to an end on October 5 of that year. The Browns defeated Pittsburgh

27-24—highlighted by Gerald "The Ice Cube" McNeil's 100-yard kickoff return for a touchdown—the first of four straight wins in what will forever be known as their own personal "House of Horrors."

23. Dave Logan. I was a third-round draft choice in 1976 from the University of Colorado. After serving primarily in a backup role my first two seasons from 1976-77, I was a starter for the most part. In 1978 I had 37 receptions for 585 yards with four touchdowns. The next year I led the Browns with 59 receptions and 982 receiving yards, and I also had seven touchdown receptions. In our season-opening 25-22 overtime victory against the Jets at Shea Stadium I caught six passes for 115 yards. I also had two good games against Pittsburgh—a five-reception, 91-yard, two-touchdown day in a 51-35 loss on October 7 at home and a seven-catch, 135-yard, one-touchdown day in a 33-30 loss on November 25 on the road.

Dub Jones in preseason action, 1951. (The Cleveland Press Collection, Michael Schwartz Library, Cleveland State University)

In our AFC Central Division championship season of 1980 I had 51 receptions for a team-leading 822 yards with four touchdowns. Included was an eight-reception, 131-yard day on October 26 in a 27-26 home win over the Steelers. My stats regressed a bit the next two years that produced losing records, but as our 1983 team improved to 9-7, my stats improved right along with it—37 receptions for 627 yards with two touchdowns, including an eight-catch, 121-yard performance in a 30-24 overtime win at San Diego. I was traded to the Denver Broncos on April 26, 1984. Overall, I had 262 receptions for 4,247 yards with 24 touchdowns.

24. Jones broke the team record, and tied the NFL mark, for most touchdowns in one game. Jones, a halfback, scored six touchdowns in a 42-21 victory over the Bears. With Marion Motley slowed down by knee problems, he stepped in—or, for that matter, took over—at least on that Sunday afternoon in Cleveland Municipal Stadium.

Jones's remarkable feat helped the Browns improve to 8-1 en route to a second straight American Conference title. Jones's six touchdowns broke the team record of four, set by Dante Lavelli on October 14, 1949, when each of Lavelli's scores came on receptions in a 61-14 rout of the Los Angeles Dons. Jones matched the feat of fullback Ernie Nevers, who totaled six touchdown catches on November 28, 1929, when he led the Chicago Cardinals to a 40-6 thumping of the crosstown Bears on Thanksgiving Day.

Whereas Lavelli and Nevers scored their touchdowns on receptions alone, Jones, who was traded from Brooklyn in 1948, tallied his by way of both the air and the ground, scoring four on runs and two on catches. Even more remarkably, all six touchdowns came in the final three quarters (Bears halfback Gale Sayers equaled Jones's and Nevers's accomplishment on December 12, 1965, when he scored six touchdowns—four rushing, one receiving, and one on a punt return—in a 61-20 drubbing of the 49ers at Wrigley Field).

After a scoreless first quarter in the Browns' victory over the Bears, Jones dove into the end zone from two yards out in the second quarter for his first touchdown, capping a 34-yard drive. Soon after, he scored on a 34-yard pass from Otto Graham to give the Browns a 14-0 halftime lead. Jones had just scratched the surface, however. In the third quarter he scored on runs of 12 and 27 yards, respectively, the second of which he started left but made a dazzling cut to the right that completely crossed up the Bears' defense. The fourth quarter brought more of the same as Jones broke free on a 43-yard run down the right sideline for his fifth touchdown of the day.

With equaling Nevers's record now a distinct possibility and the game well in hand—the Browns led 35-7—Paul Brown, Cleveland's no-nonsense head coach from the old school, did the unthinkable. When assistant coach Blanton Collier relayed down to the sideline and told Brown that Jones was just one touchdown within tying Nevers's mark, Brown allowed Jones to have a chance to do it. And do it he did, in the form of a 43-yard scoring strike from Graham for touchdown number six.

Jones might have had an opportunity to break the record but, to avoid any sort of senseless injury, Brown removed his sudden star from the game, which featured an abundance of rough play on both sides. Things got so dirty, in fact, that the Browns and Bears set single-game NFL records that still stand for most penalties against both teams (37) and most yards penalized against both teams (374). In addition, the Browns set the single-game record that has since been broken for most yards penalized against one team (209). Several players had to be helped off the field; Graham suffered a broken nose. The fact that Jones was able to accomplish what he did in such an intense game only further indicates what kind of day it was for him. What made his achievement even more amazing was that the last five times he touched the ball, he scored. He wound up with 116 yards rushing on nine carries and 80 yards receiving on three catches.

A Pro Bowler in 1951, Jones led the Browns with 492 rushing yards and 12 touchdowns. He caught 30 passes for 570 yards, including an 81-yard touchdown reception from Graham in the season opener at San Francisco. Jones played with the Browns through 1955, retiring after that season.

25. Houston Oilers. Dieken, a sixth-round draft choice in 1971 from the University of Illinois who was the starting left offen-sive tackle from early that season through 1984, caught a 14-yard touchdown pass from Paul McDonald on a fake field goal late in the first half of a 25-19 overtime win on October 30, 1983, in Cleveland. The Browns entered 4-4, Houston 0-8. The home team took a 3-0 first-quarter lead on a 37-yard field goal by Matt Bahr. It would be the Browns' only lead of the game until sudden death. Later in the first quarter the Oilers forged ahead 7-3 on a 19-yard touchdown pass from Gifford Nielsen to Mike Renfro. Florian Kempf's 19-yard second-quarter field

Doug Dieken catches a 14-yard touchdown pass from Paul McDonald on a fake field goal in a 25-19 overtime win against Houston, October 30, 1983. (AndersonsCleveland-Design.com)

goal upped their lead to 10-3, but Dieken's score tied the game 10-10 at the half.

In the third quarter Nielsen and Renfro hooked up again, this time on a 38-yard touchdown pass that put Houston back in the lead 16-10. Bahr hit another 37-yard field goal, but before the quarter was done, Kempf knocked one home from 24 yards as the Oilers not only took a 19-13 lead but also upset aspirations into the final period. Bahr kicked field goals of 29 and 30 yards to send the game into overtime. Boyce Green's 20-yard touchdown run was the winning score.

As for Dieken, who had been a Pro Bowler in 1980, he still holds Browns records of 194 straight starts and 203 consecutive games played.

PRO BOWL LEVEL

These 25 questions are for you Browns fans who are awfully astute when it comes to the history of the franchise. Go for it!

1. What year did the "Dawg Pound" originate? *Answer on page 95.*

    a. 1983   b. 1984

    c. 1985   d. 1986

2. When the Browns upset the New Orleans Saints on October 24, 2010, it marked the third straight season they beat the defending Super Bowl champion. True or false? *Answer on page 96.*

3. How many winning seasons did the Browns have in the 1970s? *Answer on page 98.*

4. Tim Couch kept the Browns' realistic playoff hopes alive when he completed a 50-yard Hail Mary touchdown pass to Quincy Morgan with no time left to give them a 21-20 triumph over the Jaguars in Jacksonville on December 8, _____. *Answer on page 103.*

    a. 1999   b. 2001

    c. 2002   d. 2007

5. The Browns have beaten both Super Bowl participants in the same season once. What year did they accomplish this unusual feat? *Answer on page 104.*

6. Milt Plum led the NFL in passing each season from 1960-61. True or false? *Answer on page 105.*

7. I was Mike Phipps's backup in 1973. I had been mainly a reserve for Green Bay and Denver prior to that. Who am I? *Answer on page 106.*

8. Name all 19 head coaches in Browns history. *Answer on page 107.*

9. I caught a 38-yard touchdown pass from Mike Phipps for the winning touchdown with 41 seconds left to give the Browns a crucial 21-17 Monday night victory over the Chargers in San Diego on November 13, 1972. My initials are F.P. Who am I? *Answer on page 112.*

10. Match the players on the left with the years they were drafted on the right. *Answer on page 113.*

Doug Dieken	1975
Dick Ambrose	1968
Mike Phipps	1971
John Garlington	1970

11. What NFL record did Jim Brown set in a 38-31 victory over the Colts at Baltimore on November 1, 1959? *Answer on page 115.*

12. Had the Browns beaten the Oakland Raiders in their Red Right 88 AFC Divisional Playoff loss on January 4, 1981, what team would they have played next? *Answer on page 116.*

13. I rushed for 137 yards despite a 44-17 defeat to the Steelers at Pittsburgh on October 16, 1983, becoming the first visiting running back to rush for 100 yards in

Three Rivers Stadium in six years. My initials are B.G. Who am I? *Answer on page 117.*

14. What was the only losing season the Browns had from 1946-73? *Answer on page 118.*
    a. 1952   b. 1956
    c. 1961   d. 1970

15. In which five seasons have the Browns come within one win of playing in the Super Bowl? *Answer on page 119.*

16. The Browns and Bengals' first-ever meeting was a preseason game on August 29, 1970, at Riverfront Stadium in Cincinnati. The Bengals won 31-14. Later in the 1970s the two teams squared off in preseason games for three consecutive years in Ohio Stadium on the campus of Ohio State University in Columbus. What years were they? *Answer on page 124.*
    a. 1974, 1975, 1976
    b. 1973, 1974, 1975
    c. 1975, 1976, 1977
    d. 1972, 1973, 1974

17. How many times did the Browns play in the Chicago College All-Star Game? *Answer on page 127.*

18. What defensive lineman intercepted a Lynn Dickey pass and returned it seven yards for a touchdown against the Green Bay Packers on November 6, 1983? *Answer on page 129.*
    a. Reggie Camp
    b. Elvis Franks
    c. Keith Baldwin
    d. Bob Golic

19. I caught a 64-yard touchdown pass from Brian Sipe in a 30-17 home win over Pittsburgh on December 18, 1983. My initials are R.B. Who am I? *Answer on page 129.*

20. In which year's season opener did the Browns' "Dwayne Rudd Helmet Toss" defeat occur? *Answer on page 130.*
a. 2001   b. 2002
c. 2003   d. 2004

21. The Browns have beaten Bill Belichick's New England Patriots twice. One was when they upset them 34-14 on November 7, 2010, in Cleveland. What was the other time? *Answer on page 132.*

22. The Browns played to a 33-33 tie with the _____ in the 1964 home opener. *Answer on page 133.*

23. I was a fullback who led the Browns in 1970 with 40 receptions and 11 touchdowns and tied for the team lead with four touchdown catches. Who am I? *Answer on page 134.*

24. How many times have the Browns finished with a .500 record? *Answer on page 135.*
a. One   b. Two
c. Three   d. Four

25. Who is Cleveland's all-time interceptions leader? *Answer on page 138.*

PRO BOWL LEVEL – ANSWERS

1. b. 1984. With the Browns at the tail end of a disheartening 5-11 season, there wasn't much for fans to cheer. During a home game, Hanford Dixon and Frank Minnifield decided to ham it up a bit and began barking—yes, barking—to fans in the bleachers section in order to liven things up. Little did the Browns' starting cornerbacks know that their woofing would be the start of quite possibly the largest, loudest, longest-running canine commotion this side of the motion picture *101 Dalmations.* Although self-proclaimed "Top Dawg" Dixon and "Mighty Minnie" Minnifield were the first to fire up the bleacher-goers, it was linebacker Eddie Johnson who started the whole Dawg phenomenon by barking at defensive mates when they would make a big hit or play aggressively.

Legions of fans in the bleachers section not only barked their lungs out but also attired themselves in dog masks and painted their faces brown, orange, and white. Some even feasted on dog biscuits! If someone completely oblivious to Cleveland Browns football had walked into Cleveland Stadium during a game at this time and saw what was going on in the bleachers, they probably would have thought to themselves, *What's a dog pound doing in a football stadium?* Well, that's exactly what the bleachers section had become—a Dawg Pound, which is what it came to be known not only in Cleveland but nationwide. The creation of the Dawg Pound soon coincided with the team's new winning ways after suffering losing records in three of the previous four seasons, which increased the barking even more. Even during the mostly less-than-mediocre seasons in the early 1990s, the Dawg Pound continued its crazy canine antics.

When the expansion Browns of 1999 arrived three years after the original Browns skipped town to Baltimore, The Dawg Pound was reborn as the official name of the Cleveland Browns Stadium (now FirstEnergy Stadium) bleachers section. Although enthusiastic, this Dawg Pound certainly lacks the charm and madness of the original Dawg Pound, in which fans became a little too enthusiastic at times as several "Canine Quarterbacks" would hurl biscuits, batteries, and eggs, among other inanimate objects, at opposing players. Their rowdiness made life so miserable for opposing teams that, at one point during a victory over the Denver Broncos in 1989, officials were forced to move play to the closed end of the stadium. But, all in all, the positives outweighed the negatives, and the Cleveland Stadium bleachers section will forever be known as the pound that knew how to party.

2. True. They beat the New York Giants in 2008 and the Pittsburgh Steelers in 2009. The game against the Giants, who had beaten New England in Super Bowl XLII, was on Monday Night Football in Cleveland Browns Stadium. New York entered with a 4-0 record, the Browns 1-3. The game was close for the first three quarters. Phil Dawson's 28-yard field goal gave the home team a 3-0 lead after one quarter, but Brandon Jacobs's seven-yard touchdown run in the second quarter gave the Giants a 7-3 lead. Just more than a minute later the Browns forged back ahead 10-7 on Jamal Lewis's four-yard touchdown run. They upped their lead to 17-7 later in the quarter when

Derek Anderson threw a 22-yard touchdown pass to Darnell Dinkins. Eli Manning's three-yard touchdown pass to Plaxico Burress with just 12 seconds left in the quarter cut the deficit to 17-14 at halftime.

Dawson's 26-yard third-quarter field goal increased the Cleveland lead to 20-14 entering the final period. The fourth quarter was all Browns. First, Anderson hit Braylon Edwards on an 11-yard touchdown pass. Then about midway through the fourth Eric Wright intercepted a pass by Manning and returned it 94 yards for a touchdown for the game's final points as the Browns shocked the nation by winning 35-14.

Anderson was 18-of-29 for 310 yards with the two touchdowns. Lewis ran the ball 21 times for 88 yards with the touchdown. Edwards had five receptions for 154 yards, including a 70-yarder from Anderson, with the touchdown. Manning was 18-of-28 for 196 yards with the touchdown and three interceptions; he was sacked once. Derrick Ward rushed the ball 10 times for 101 yards, while Jacobs had 14 carries for 67 yards with the touchdown. Steve Smith had nine receptions for 94 yards, while Burress had four catches for 58 yards with the touchdown.

The Steelers game was on Thursday night, December 10, at Cleveland. Pittsburgh, which had defeated Arizona in Super Bowl XLIII, entered the game with a 6-6 record and in desperate need of a victory in regards to the AFC playoff race. The Browns came in just 1-11. The game was a defensive battle. Two field goals by Phil Dawson and two by Jeff Reed sandwiched a 10-yard touchdown run by Chris Jennings late in the first half in the Browns' 13-6 upset win.

Brady Quinn was 6-of-19 for 90 yards, including a 37-yarder to Mohamed Massaquoi, and was sacked once.

Jennings had 20 rushes for 73 yards with the touchdown. Ben Roethlisberger was 18-of-32 for 201 yards and was sacked eight times. Santonio Holmes caught six passes for 93 yards.

The game against the Saints was played in the Superdome. The Browns came in with a 1-5 record, the Saints 4-2. New Orleans dominated 25-12 in first downs and 394-210 in total yards, but turnovers were the difference—the Saints had four, the Browns none. Cleveland was up 13-3 late in the first half when David Bowens picked off Drew Brees and returned the ball 30 yards for a touchdown and a 20-3 lead at the half. Bowens did it again with 3:33 to go in the game when he turned another Brees pass into a 64-yard pick-six to increase the Browns' lead to 30-10, nailing the coffin door shut on the Saints in a 30-17 shocker.

Colt McCoy was 9-of-16 for 74 yards and was sacked once. Peyton Hillis rushed the ball 16 times for 69 yards with a touchdown. Brees was 37-of-56 for 356 yards with two touchdowns and four interceptions. He was sacked three times. Marques Colston had 10 receptions for 112 yards with a touchdown.

3. Five. They had winning seasons from 1971-73 and in 1976 and 1979. Under first-year head coach Nick Skorich, the 1971 Browns won four of their first five games. The offense took a hiatus as they scored just 30 combined points in successive defeats to the Broncos, Falcons, Steelers, and Chiefs. A 27-7 home win over New England, however, sparked a five-game winning streak to end the season, earning the 9-5 Browns the AFC Central Division title and a matchup with Baltimore in the divisional playoffs. The visiting Colts, led by an aging but still savvy John Unitas, easily beat Cleveland 20-3 the day after Christmas.

Skorich alternated between Bill Nelsen and third-year quarterback Mike Phipps during the 1972 preseason. But after the Browns lost to Green Bay in the opener with the two splitting the playing time, the coach inserted Phipps, the former Purdue University star, as the starter for Game 2 in Philadelphia. Phipps passed for a touchdown and scored one himself in leading the Browns to a 27-17 victory, and in the process, received Skorich's stamp of approval to be the starter for the rest of the season.

After an easy win over the Bengals, the Browns lost two in a row to drop to 2-3, but six straight wins ensued, including thrillers over the Chargers and Steelers, the former a 21-17 Monday nighter and the latter 26-24 on a late field goal by Don Cockroft that forged a tie between them and Pittsburgh for the Central Division lead with both teams 7-3. Two weeks later the Browns and Steelers squared off again—this time, though, in Pittsburgh. With both teams 8-3, the outright division lead was at stake. The Browns were limited to 27 yards passing and were manhandled 30-0. Pittsburgh won its final two games to nail down the division championship—its first title of any kind in 40 years of competition—finishing 11-3. The Browns, also winners of their last two, wound up 10-4, good enough for the AFC's wild card berth, and were rewarded with a trip down south to face the unbeaten Miami Dolphins in the divisional playoffs.

The Browns threw a huge scare at the heavily favored Dolphins and, when Phipps threw a 27-yard touchdown pass to Fair Hooker, had a one-point lead early in the fourth quarter. Miami bounced back, though, and sealed a 20-14 victory when late in the game linebacker Doug Swift intercepted a Phipps pass, the young quarterback's fifth pick of the day, deep in Dolphins territory.

With Nelsen retired and Phipps still at the controls, Cleveland looked to be headed for the playoffs again in 1973 when on November 25 rookie Greg Pruitt dashed 19 yards for a touchdown late in the game to give the Browns a 21-16 victory over the Steelers at home. The next week at Kansas City, the speedster from the University of Oklahoma, a second-round draft pick in 1973, scored on a 65-yard run as the Browns rallied from a 14-point fourth-quarter deficit to tie the Chiefs. That left them with a 7-3-2 record and a virtual share of first place with Cincinnati and Pittsburgh, both 8-4. A 34-17 pounding at the hands of the Bengals, though, finished the Browns for all intents and purposes. They wound up 7-5-2 and in third place.

In 1976 Phipps held off a challenge from two-year backup Brian Sipe in training camp and was the starter when the season began. After passing for three second-quarter touchdowns in leading the Browns to a 21-10 halftime lead against the New York Jets in the opener at home, Phipps suffered a separated shoulder early in the third quarter. Sipe came in and put the finishing touches on a 38-17 triumph by tossing touchdown passes to Reggie Rucker and Steve Holden. Blowout losses to Pittsburgh, Denver, and Cincinnati followed, but Sipe was beginning to solidify himself as the starter.

Third-string quarterback Dave Mays, a World Football League refugee, was the hero a week later as the Browns began a huge turnaround with a stunning upset of the two-time defending Super Bowl Champion Steelers in Cleveland Municipal Stadium. Though not spectacular, Mays did what was needed in replacing Sipe, who was knocked out of the game in the second quarter. Defensive end Joe "Turkey" Jones put the stamp on Cleveland's fine defensive effort early in the fourth quarter by not only sacking Terry Bradshaw but lifting him up and slamming him head first to the ground. Bradshaw would miss the next two games due to back and neck injuries suffered on the play.

With Sipe back the next week, the Browns beat the Falcons and lost just one more game entering the season's final week. Tied with the Steelers and Bengals at 9-4 but in the precarious position in which they would lose out in tiebreakers to both teams, the Browns knew the only way they could qualify for the postseason was by winning the AFC Central outright (they had no shot at the AFC's wild card berth). But before they even took the field for their finale in Kansas City, their division title dreams, as faint as they were, had been shattered by Pittsburgh's 20-0 victory over Houston the day before. The Browns played like it, too, in an embarrassing 39-14 loss to the lowly Chiefs. They still finished 9-5, though, in third place, a game behind the division champion Steelers and also the Bengals, who, like Pittsburgh, finished 10-4 but lost out on the division crown due to their two defeats to the Steelers during the season.

Joe "Turkey" Jones slams Terry Bradshaw to the ground during an 18-16 upset of Pittsburgh, October 10, 1976. (AndersonsCleve-landDesign.com)

After having flirted with late-game heroics the year before, the Browns, under second-year head coach Sam Rutigliano, made a habit of it and became known as the Kardiac Kids in 1979. After three nail-biting victories to open the season, they routed the defending NFC champion Dallas Cowboys— "America's Team"—26-7 under the bright lights of *Monday Night Football* on September 24 in a rocking Cleveland Stadium to improve to 4-0. The Browns split their next eight games, two of which were pulse-pounding victories over contenders Philadelphia and Miami, the latter of which upped their record to 8-4, leaving them a game behind Pittsburgh and Houston with a trip down the turnpike set for seven days later.

The Browns invaded Three Rivers Stadium on November 25 and led by scores of 20-6, 27-13, and 30-20, which slowly disappeared. The defending Super Bowl Champion Steelers hung a 33-30 heartbreaker on the visitors when future Brown Matt Bahr kicked a 37-yard field goal with nine seconds left in sudden death. The next week in the home finale, Mike Pruitt outgained the awesome Earl Campbell as the Browns beat the Oilers in the snow to improve to 9-5. Cleveland's postseason dreams received a crushing blow seven days later, however, with a 19-14 defeat to wild-card rival Oakland on the West Coast.

The Browns entered the final weekend of the season with a 9-6 record. They needed a win in Cincinnati on the final Sunday, and losses by the Raiders (also 9-6) later that day to Seattle and Denver (10-5) the following night in San Diego, in order to overtake the two AFC West rivals for the second and final conference wild card berth (a Raiders tie would have been sufficient, as well).

The scenario with Oakland was simple. The Raiders, due to their victory over the Browns the previous week, owned the head-to-head tiebreaker over Cleveland, meaning the Browns had to finish with a better record than them. Matters were a touch more confusing when it came to the situation with Denver. Due to the complicated tiebreaking formula, the combined points differential in the Browns' win over the Bengals and the Broncos' loss to the Chargers would have had to total 43 points, which would have put the Browns in a tie with Denver in net points in AFC games. In that scenario, the Browns would have won the next tiebreaker, which was net points in all games.

Although Oakland did its part by losing to the Seahawks and the Broncos did their part (somewhat) by falling to the Chargers (by only 10 points, though), the tiebreaking scenarios went for naught because the Browns had already lost 16-12 to the lowly Bengals when Ricky Feacher had a fourth-down pass from Sipe ricochet off his fingertips in the Cincinnati end zone in the final minute (in retrospect, however, the Browns would have had to defeat the Bengals by at least 33 points to qualify for the playoffs). The Browns finished 9-7 and in third place in the Central Division, behind division champion Pittsburgh and Houston, which earned the AFC's first wild card berth.

4. c. 2002. The Browns entered the game 6-6 and coming off an embarrassing home loss to a Carolina team that had dropped eight games in a row. The Jaguars came in with a 5-7 record. Jacksonville took a 7-0 first-quarter lead when Mark Brunell hit Kyle Brady on a four-yard touchdown pass. The score stayed the same until midway through the third quarter when William Green tied the game on a three-yard touchdown run. The Jags forged back ahead 14-7 on a 44-yard touchdown run by Fred Taylor. Less than two minutes later Couch hit Morgan on a long touchdown pass, this one a 60-yarder, to tie the game at 14 heading into the fourth quarter. Two Danny Boyd field goals late in the game gave the Jags a 20-14 lead. Then came Couch's game-winning pass to Morgan.

Couch was 21-of-35 for 264 yards with the two touchdowns and two interceptions and was sacked three times. Green rushed the ball 26 times for 119 yards with the touchdown and had three receptions for 25 yards. Morgan caught three passes for 118 yards with the two touchdowns. Brunell was 10-of-14 for 73 yards with the touchdown and was sacked three times. Taylor had 23 carries for 145 yards with the touchdown.

5. 1981. They defeated the Cincinnati Bengals and San Francisco 49ers. Even more remarkable is that they were just 5-11 that season. On top of that, both games were on the road! The Browns beat Cincinnati 20-17 on September 20. They came in 0-2, the Bengals 2-0. Two Dave Jacobs field goals and a four-yard touchdown pass from Brian Sipe to Ozzie Newsome gave Cleveland a 13-0 halftime lead. The Bengals cut it to 13-10 on a 21-yard Jim Breech field goal in the third quarter and a 41-yard touchdown strike from Ken Anderson to Cris Collinsworth in the fourth quarter. Mike Pruitt upped the Browns' lead to 20-10 with a 12-yard touchdown run. Pete Johnson scored from a yard out for the final points.

Sipe was 24-of-35 for 259 yards with the touchdown and was sacked twice. Cleo Miller rushed the ball 22 times for 96 yards and had three receptions for 24 yards, while Pruitt had 13 carries for 70 yards with the touchdown and three catches for 20 yards. Charles White had seven receptions for 73 yards, and Reggie Rucker had two catches for 63 yards, including a 49-yarder from Sipe. Anderson was 16-of-25 for 238 yards with the touchdown; he was sacked once. Isaac Curtis had four receptions for 79 yards, including a 44-yarder from Anderson, while Collinsworth caught three passes for 66 yards with the touchdown.

Eight weeks later, on November 15, the Browns beat San Francisco 15-12. They were 4-6 entering the game, and the 49ers, on their way to victory in Super Bowl XVI, were 8-2. Four field goals by Ray Wersching and one by Matt Bahr plus a Cleveland safety added up to a 12-5 Niners lead after three quarters. The game's only touchdown was when Sipe hit Rucker on a 21-yard pass, tying the score at 12. Bahr kicked a 24-yard field goal to win the game.

Sipe was 16-of-33 for 180 yards with the touchdown and an interception and was sacked twice. Pruitt carried the ball 18 times for 76 yards. Rucker had three receptions for 77 yards, including a 38-yarder, with the touchdown. Joe Montana was 24-of-42 for 213 yards with two interceptions and was sacked three times. Paul Hofer had seven receptions for 64 yards, and Dwight Clark had six catches for 52 yards.

6. False. Plum led the league in passer rating in 1960 only. A Pro Bowler both years, he was a second-round draft pick in 1957 from Penn State University and played for the Browns from 1957-61. In 1960 he had a 110.4 passer rating, an NFL record that stood until Joe Montana broke it 29 years later, completing 151 of 250 attempts for 2,297 yards with 21 touchdowns and just five interceptions. He had several great performances. One was on October 23 against the Eagles when he was 16-of-22 for 289 yards with two touchdowns, including an 86-yarder to Leon Clarke. Another was three weeks later in a 28-27 win over St. Louis when he was 11-of-15 for 194 yards with two touchdowns, including a 66-yarder to Ray Renfro.

In 1961 Plum had a 90.3 passer rating, completing 177 of 302 attempts for 2,416 yards with 18 touchdowns and 10 interceptions. In a season-opening loss to the Eagles in Philadelphia he was 18-of-30 for 329 yards with two touchdowns, including a 60-yarder to Charley Ferguson, and an interception. Two months later, on November 19 in a 45-24 victory over the same Eagles (but in Cleveland), he was 16-of-21 for 246 yards with a touchdown. He was traded to the Lions in the off-season. Overall, he completed 627 of 1,083 passes for 8,914 yards with 66 touchdowns and 39 interceptions.

7. Don Horn. I saw very little action in 1973, my only year with the Browns. I completed four of eight passes for 22 yards with a touchdown. My scoring pass was a two-yarder to Bo Scott in mop-up duty during a 42-13 rout of the Houston Oilers at Cleveland Municipal Stadium.

As a rookie with the soon-to-be two-time defending Super Bowl Champion Packers in 1967, I completed 12 of 24 passes for 171 yards with a touchdown and an interception. In 1968 with Green Bay I completed 10 of 16 passes for 187 yards with two touchdowns. The next season with the Packers I started five games and completed 89 of 168 passes for 1,505 yards with 11 touchdowns and 11 picks. In the season finale I was 22-of-31 for 410 yards with five touchdowns and an interception in a 45-28 win over St. Louis. In 1970, my final season with Green Bay, I completed 28 of 76 passes for 428 yards with just two touchdowns and 10 interceptions.

In my first season with Denver in 1971 I started nine games and completed 89 of 173 passes for 1,056 yards with only three touchdowns and 14 interceptions. In a 34-13 Week 2 loss to my former team, the Packers, I was horrible—16-of-33 for 186 yards with six interceptions. I saw no action with the Broncos in 1972 nor any in my final season of 1974 with the Chargers.

8. Paul Brown, Blanton Collier, Nick Skorich, Forrest Gregg, Dick Modzelewski, Sam Rutigliano, Marty Schottenheimer, Bud Carson, Jim Shofner, Bill Belichick, Chris Palmer, Butch Davis, Terry Robiskie, Romeo Crennel, Eric Mangini, Pat Shurmur, Rob Chudzinski, Mike Pettine, and Hue Jackson.

Brown was Cleveland's first head coach, beginning with the franchise's first season in 1946. His surname is the reason behind the team's nickname; he is the only pro football coach for whom a team has been named. Brown led Cleveland to four straight championships in the AAFC from 1946-49 and six straight title-game appearances in the NFL from 1950-55, plus another in 1957. His team won three of those games (1950 and from 1954-55).

An innovator when it came to football, Brown was the first head coach to hire a full-time coaching staff, utilize classroom study to such a broad extent, use intelligence tests, grade his players from individual film clips, and develop a messenger-guard system so he could call plays from the sideline. He had much to do with inventing, or improving, plays such as the screen pass, draw play, and trap plays. He also invented the first single-bar facemask.

Brown's days as head football coach and athletic officer at the Great Lakes Naval Training Center had much to do with his firing by Art Modell on January 9, 1963. Toward the end of his reign as head coach many players, including Jim Brown, were growing tired of his military-like approach to dealing with them. They also believed the game was passing him by, that his play-calling had become too conservative for the changing times. Furthermore, he was constantly in disagreement with Modell over how the team should be run. His overall record was 158-48-8. He was inducted into the Pro Football Hall of Fame in 1967.

Collier, the offensive backfield coach under Brown in 1962, replaced the living legend and opened up the offense as Cleveland improved to 10-4 after going 7-6-1 the year before. He led the Browns to the NFL Championship the next year in upsetting the Baltimore Colts 27-0 in the title game. Under Collier, the Browns played in three more NFL Championship games, in 1965 and from 1968-69. He retired after the 1970 season. His overall record was 76-34-2.

Skorich, Collier's offensive coordinator in 1970, replaced him. He led the Browns to 9-5 and 10-4 records in 1971 and 1972, respectively. The 1971 team won the AFC Central Division, and the 1972 team qualified for the playoffs as the AFC's wild card entrant. Both years, the Browns were ousted in the divisional playoffs, by Baltimore in 1971 and Miami in 1972. Until Mangini in 2009, Skorich was the only Browns head coach who had prior NFL head-coaching experience (with the Philadelphia Eagles from 1961-63). He was fired on December 12, 1974, but finished the season in a loss at Houston. His overall record was 30-24-2.

Gregg, the offensive line coach under Skorich in 1974, took over for him. He began his first season 0-9 en route to a 3-11 last-place finish. The Browns improved to 9-5 in 1976, missing the playoffs on the final weekend. The team started the 1977 season 5-2 but lost six of its last seven games to finish 6-8 and in last place. Gregg was fired with one game left. His overall record was 18-23. Modzelewski, the defensive coordinator under Gregg in 1977, replaced him on an interim basis for the final game, a 20-19 loss at Seattle.

Rutigliano was the new head coach in 1978. He led the Browns to some exciting times in both 1979 and 1980. His Kardiac Kids won several games (and lost some, too) in thrilling fashion during that period. His 1980 team won the Central Division title but lost to Oakland 14-12 in the Red Right 88 divisional playoff game. His 1982 club qualified for the expanded, strike-induced play-offs with a losing record and fell to the Raiders, who by then made Los Angeles their home. He was fired halfway through the 1984 season, the day after a 12-9 last-second loss to the lowly Bengals in Cincinnati dropped the team's record to 1-7. His overall record was 47-50.

Schottenheimer, Rutigliano's defensive coordinator in 1984, replaced him and led the Browns to a 4-4 finish for a 5-11 final record. He led them to Central Division titles from 1985-87 and a wild card berth in 1988. They lost heartbreaking AFC finals to Denver in 1986 and 1987. Philosophical differences with Modell led to his resignation following the 1988 season. His overall record was 44-27.

Sam Rutigliano. (Andersons ClevelandDesign.com)

Carson, a longtime defensive guru and the architect—the defensive coordinator—of Pittsburgh's vaunted "Steel Curtain" defense for five years in the 1970s, replaced Schottenheimer.

His Browns opened the 1989 season with a 51-0 destruction of the Steelers at Three Rivers Stadium. The team had its ups and downs but still finished 9-6-1 and Central Division champions. However, the season ended with another loss to the Broncos in the AFC title game. Carson was fired when the Browns lost seven of their first nine games in 1990. His overall record was 11-13-1. Shofner, his offensive coordinator in 1990, replaced Carson on an interim basis and went 1-6 for a final record of 3-13.

Belichick, the New York Giants' defensive coordinator the year before when they won Super Bowl XXV, was the new head coach in 1991. The Browns improved to 6-10 that year and 7-9 in both 1992 and 1993. Led by a stalwart defense in 1994, they went 11-5 and beat New England in a wild card game before getting pounced at Pittsburgh in the next round. Belichick was fired following a 5-11 record in 1995, a season in which Modell announced after nine games that he would be relocating the team to Baltimore the following season. Belichick's overall record was 36-44.

Palmer was the first head coach of the reincarnated, expansion Browns in 1999. They were embarrassed at home by Pittsburgh 43-0 in the season opener and finished just 2-14. The next year, they started 2-1, but a 36-10 beating at Oakland was the start of another horrific season. They finished 3-13 and were shut out four times in their last 12 games. Palmer was fired after the season. His overall record was 5-27.

Davis, the head coach at the University of Miami the previous six seasons, replaced Palmer. He led the Browns to a 6-4 start in 2001 that ended with a 7-9 record. The next year he led them to a 9-7 record, second place in the AFC North Division, and a wild card berth. They squandered a 24-7 third-quarter lead and lost 36-33 to the Steelers at Pittsburgh in the opening round of the playoffs. Both the 2003 and 2004 Browns split their first six games before plummeting to last-place finishes. Davis resigned after a 58-48 loss to the Bengals in Cincinnati on Thanksgiving weekend in 2004 dropped his team's record to 3-8. His overall record was 24-35. Terry Robiskie, his offensive coordinator in 2004, replaced him on an interim basis and finished the season by losing four of five games for a final record of 4-12.

Crennel, New England's defensive coordinator the four previous seasons that included three Super Bowl titles, took over for Robiskie as the new head coach. His 2005 and 2006 teams finished 6-10 and 4-12, respectively, but the next year improved to 10-6 and barely missed the playoffs. Crennel's last club in 2008 was perhaps his worst. Not only did the Browns finish 4-12, but they scored a total of just 31 points in their final six games—all losses, the final two shutouts. Crennel was fired after the season. His overall record was 24-40.

Mangini, the New York Jets' head coach the three previous seasons, replaced Crennel. His first team in 2009 started 1-11 but won its last four games for a 5-11 record. The next year, the Browns began 1-5, then pulled two upsets—over the Saints and Patriots. They split their next four games and were 5-7 but closed the season with four straight defeats for another 5-11 record. Mangini was fired one day after the season finale, a 41-9 home loss to the Steelers. His overall record was 10-22.

Shurmur replaced Mangini in 2011 and won two of his first three games, including a last-minute victory over Miami in Cleveland Browns Stadium. The Browns were 3-3 but finished 4-12. The 2012 team lost its first five games en route to a 5-11 record. Shurmur was fired after the season. His overall record was 9-23.

The coaching carousel continued in 2013 as Rob Chudzinski, a Browns assistant coach on two different occasions in the 2000s, replaced Shurmur. The 2013 Browns started 0-2 but won three straight, the last one a 37-24 victory over the visiting Bills on national television. Three losses ensued, but the Browns then beat Baltimore 24-18 to get to 4-5. They lost their last seven games, though, to finish 4-12 and in last place. Chudzinski was fired after the season.

Longtime NFL assistant coach Mike Pettine replaced Chudzinski. Pettine's 2014 Browns, believe it or not, were 7-4 following a thrilling, last-second 26-24 win over the Falcons in Atlanta. However, a 26-10 loss in Buffalo the next week was the start of a five-game losing streak—including some sad samples of Johnny Manziel—for a 7-9 final record. Pettine's 2015 Browns sunk to 3-13. He was fired the day of the season finale, after a 28-12 home loss to Pittsburgh. Overall, he was 10-22.

Hue Jackson replaced Pettine in 2016. The Browns produced the worst record in franchise history, finishing 1-15. They lost their first 14 games before finally cracking the win column with a 20-17 victory over San Diego on Christmas Eve before a ton of empty seats in FirstEnergy Stadium. Their win over the Chargers was the only game in which they yielded fewer than 23 points.

9. Frank Pitts. I was a wide receiver traded from Kansas City on September 8, 1971. I saw little action in my first three seasons with the Chiefs from 1965-67, but in 1968 I had 30 receptions for 655 yards with six touchdowns, including a 90-yarder from Len Dawson during a 31-17 home win over the Boston Patriots on November 17. We finished 12-2 but lost to Oakland in a divisional playoff game. The next year I had 31 receptions for 470 yards with two touchdowns as we went on to win Super Bowl IV 23-7 over Minnesota. In the win over the Vikings,

I caught three passes for 33 yards and ran the ball three times for 37 yards. In 1970, my final season with the Chiefs, I had 11 catches for 172 yards with two touchdowns.

In 1971, my first year with the Browns, I had 27 receptions for 487 yards with a team-leading four touchdowns, including a 53-yarder from Bill Nelsen in a 31-27 victory over the Bengals in Week 12, a game in which I had five receptions for 103 yards. Three weeks earlier in a loss to my old team, the Chiefs, I had five catches for 129 yards.

The next year I led the Browns with 36 receptions, 620 receiving yards, and eight touchdown catches, including an 80-yarder—one of two touchdown catches I had that day— from Mike Phipps in a 26-10 victory in the season finale over the Jets in New York, a game in which I caught four passes for 98 yards. In Week 3 that year at home against Cincinnati, a 27-6 victory, I caught four balls for 105 yards, including a 68-yard touchdown pass from Phipps. In 1973, my last season with Cleveland, I had a team-best 31 receptions for 317 yards with a team-high four touchdown catches. Overall with the Browns, I had 94 receptions for 1,424 yards with 16 touchdowns.

10. Doug Dieken, a left offensive tackle, was drafted in the sixth round in 1971 out of the University of Illinois. Dick Ambrose, a linebacker, was selected in the 12th round in 1975 from the University of Virginia. Mike Phipps, a quarterback, was a first-round pick—the third overall selection—in 1970 from Purdue University. John Garlington, a linebacker, was chosen in the second round in 1968 out of LSU.

Dieken carried on the fine tradition of left tackles when he replaced veteran Dick Schafrath during the 1971 season. He was the team's starter at that position through 1984, his last year with the Browns. Excellent at both run and pass blocking, he proved to be an outstanding player and an iron man to boot. He set team records that still stand with 194 straight starts and 203 consecutive games played. One of his more memorable moments actually came as a receiver when, on October 30, 1983, during a home win over Houston he caught a 14-yard touchdown pass from Paul McDonald on a fake field goal, the only touchdown of his career. He was a Pro Bowler in 1980.

Ambrose was known for his hard-nosed tackling. He had one fumble recovery in 1975 and two in 1977. In 1978 he had two interceptions, one of which he returned 39 yards in a Week 15 win over the Jets, plus a fumble recovery. The next season he had a pick and a fumble recovery. He had one interception and two fumble recoveries in 1981, one of each in 1982, and a fumble recovery in 1983. After spending 1984 on the injured reserve list, he retired.

To get Phipps, the Browns traded the great Paul Warfield to Miami on January 26, 1970, for the Dolphins' first-round selection, which was the third overall pick in the next day's draft. Phipps sat behind veteran Bill Nelsen for most of the 1970 and 1971 seasons. He became the full-time starter in Week 2 of 1972, which was his best season. He completed 144 of 305 passes for 1,994 yards with 13 touchdowns and 16 interceptions. The team finished 10-4 and, despite Phipps's five interceptions, took the undefeated Dolphins down to the wire in a 20-14 defeat in an AFC Divisional Playoff at the Orange Bowl.

Things went downhill from there. Phipps's touchdown passes/interceptions ratio was not exactly Pro Bowl-like the next three seasons: 9/20, 9/17, and 4/19 as the Browns finished 7-5-2, 4-10, and 3-11. He held off a challenge from Brian Sipe in the 1976 training camp and started the opening game against the New York Jets at home. He passed for three second-quarter touchdowns en route to a 21-10 halftime lead, only to suffer a separated shoulder early in the third quarter. Sipe came in and put the finishing touches on a 38-17 victory and remained the starter, leading the team to a 9-5 record. Phipps was traded to the Chicago Bears on May 3, 1977. Overall, he completed 633 of 1,317 passes for 7,700 yards with 40 touchdowns and 81 interceptions.

Garlington had one interception and two fumble recoveries in his rookie season of 1968. In 1969 he had two interceptions and two fumble recoveries. The next year he had a pick and a fumble recovery. He had an interception in both 1971 and 1972, and in 1973 he had a pick and a fumble recovery. In 1974 he had two picks, including one he returned 28 yards in a Week 2 win over Houston, and two fumble recoveries. He played with the Browns through 1977.

11. Most rushing touchdowns in one game. He had five. Cleveland entered with a 3-2 record, while Baltimore came in with a 4-1 mark. With the scored tied 3-3 in the second quarter, Brown raced for a 70-yard touchdown and a 10-3 Browns lead. The Colts tied the game at 10 on a three-yard touchdown pass from John Unitas to Lenny Moore. Brown's second touchdown was a 17-yard run that gave the visitors a 17-10 halftime lead.

Brown scored from three yards out in the third quarter to up Cleveland's lead to 24-10. Unitas hit Jerry Richardson for an eight-yard touchdown pass to make it 24-17. Brown scored on a one-yard run to give his team a 31-17 lead heading into the fourth quarter. He scored again from a yard out, which was sandwiched between two more Baltimore touchdowns. His feat has been matched twice—by Jacksonville's James Stewart against the Eagles on October 12, 1997, and by Denver's Clinton Portis against the Chiefs on December 7, 2003.

Milt Plum was 14-of-23 for 200 yards with two interceptions. Brown ran the ball 32 times for 178 yards with the five touchdowns. Bobby Mitchell had five receptions for 66 yards, Preston Carpenter had three receptions for 56 yards, Billy Howton had three catches for 48 yards, and Ray Renfro caught two passes for 30 yards. Unitas was 23-of-41 for 397 yards with four touchdowns and three interceptions. Raymond Berry had 11 receptions for 156 yards with a touchdown, Moore had five catches for 115 yards, including a 71-yarder from Unitas, with the touchdown, and Jim Mutscheller had four receptions for 84 yards, including a 40-yarder from Unitas, with a touchdown.

12. San Diego Chargers. This dreamy matchup between the Kardiac Kids and "Air Coryell" would have taken place the next week, on January 11 in San Diego, in the AFC Championship game. The following are four other "Coulda-Been Matchups That Woulda Been Great:"

*Browns vs. New York Giants (Super Bowl XXI, January 25, 1987, at Pasadena, California)
-Two franchises whose storied rivalry in the 1950s and early 1960s was one of the fiercest could have made their initial Super Bowl appearances against one another, but Denver's "drive" to Pasadena ruined it.
*Denver at Browns (September 28, 1987)
-The Browns had been waiting for this—a rematch of the AFC Championship nine months earlier—ever since the schedule

was released the previous spring. The game, to have been show-cased on *Monday Night Football,* was the one game the entire city of Cleveland had hungered for—but also the one game cancelled by the players' strike.

*Pittsburgh at Browns (AFC Championship, January 14, 1990) -If not for a touch of John Elway magic the week before, this salivating matchup would have occurred.

*Miami at Browns (AFC Wild Card Playoff, January 1, 1995) -Had the Dolphins lost to the Lions in their regular-season finale the week before, Bernie Kosar's return to Cleveland—albeit as Dan Marino's backup—would have been compa-rable, at least in terms of newsworthiness, to the release of Kosar the previous season (just think if Marino had gone down!).

13. Boyce Green. An 11th-round draft choice in 1983 from Carson-Newman University, I accumulated that yardage total on 28 carries, including 23- and one-yard touchdowns. I also had five receptions for 35 yards. It was a game in which we led in just about every category except turnovers. They had two, and we had seven, six of which were interceptions by Brian Sipe and one of which was a fumble by me that Greg Best returned 94 yards for a touchdown.

Sipe was 27-of-49 for 310 yards with the six picks and was sacked twice. Ozzie Newsome had nine receptions for 103 yards, while Bobby Jones caught six passes for 88 yards. Cliff Stoudt was 14-of-18 for 194 yards with a touchdown and was sacked once. Walter Abercrombie rushed the ball 15 times for 65 yards with a touchdown and had three receptions for 27 yards. Calvin Sweeney had four catches for 69 yards, including a 40-yarder for a touchdown from Stoudt.

Two weeks later in a 25-19 overtime win against Houston, I ran the ball 14 times for 107 yards, including the game-winning 20-yarder, and caught four passes for 40 yards. For the season, in which we were 9-7 and just missed the playoffs, I rushed for 497 yards on 104 carries with three touchdowns and had 25 receptions for 167 yards with a touchdown. I also returned 17 kickoffs for 350 yards.

I had both a team-leading 202 carries and 673 yards rushing in 1984 and had 12 receptions for 124 yards, including a 44-yard touchdown catch from Paul McDonald in a Week 4 win over Pittsburgh. On November 4 I amassed 156 yards on 29 carries in a 13-10 win over the Bills at Buffalo. Two weeks later in a 23-7 victory at Atlanta I ran the ball 30 times for 121 yards. My final season was 1985. Overall, I had 306 rushes for 1,170 yards with three touchdowns and 37 receptions for 291 yards with two touchdowns.

14. b. 1956. They finished 5-7 and tied for fourth place in the Eastern Conference. With Otto Graham retired, the Browns, after 10 straight seasons of championship-game appearances, finally faltered. They had a 7-6 lead in the fourth quarter but fell 9-7 to the Cardinals at Chicago in the season opener on September 30. The next week against the Steelers in Pittsburgh, it was tight from start to finish. The Browns took a 7-0 second-quarter lead on a one-yard touchdown run by George Ratterman. The Steelers answered with a 30-yard field goal by Gary Glick and a one-yard touchdown run by Lynn Chandnois as they took a 10-7 halftime lead. Ed Modzelewski's 13-yard touchdown run in the fourth quarter were the final points in a 14-10 victory.

Three defeats followed—a 21-9 home loss to the New York Giants, a 20-9 loss at Washington, and a 24-16 home loss to the Steelers—to drop Cleveland's record to 1-4. In the loss to the Giants, Alex Webster scored three touchdowns—two rushing and one receiving—while Modzelewski scored the Browns' only touchdown, a one-yard run in the second quarter. In the loss to the Redskins, it was close until the fourth quarter. The Browns were up 3-0, the Redskins were up 7-3 and then 7-6, and the Browns led again, 9-7 at the half. Washington forged ahead for good 14-9 in the third quarter when Eddie LeBaron hit Dick James on a nine-yard touchdown pass. Two field goals by future Brown Sam Baker in the fourth quarter put the game away. In the loss to the Steelers, the Browns squandered an early 13-0 lead by yielding three touchdowns in the second quarter—a one-yard run by Chandnois sandwiched by 10- and 75-yard passes, respectively, from Ted Marchibroda to Elbie Nickel and Lowell Perry.

The Browns then traveled to Milwaukee and easily beat the Packers 24-7, which was highlighted by a 39-yard fumble return for a touchdown by Chuck Noll that gave them a 7-0 first-quarter lead. They returned home the next week and lost 21-7 to the Colts before defeating the Eagles 16-0 in Philadelphia to get to 3-5. They fell 20-17 to the Redskins at home before winning two straight games for the only time all year, a 17-14 victory at home over Philadelphia and a 24-7 upset of the Giants in New York. The Browns failed in their bid for a .500 season by losing 24-7 to the visiting Cardinals, a disappointing end to a disappointing season.

15. 1968, 1969, 1986, 1987, and 1989. In 1968 the Browns finished 10-4, won the Century Division, and upset Dallas 31-20 at home in the Eastern Conference championship game before getting blown out 34-0 by Baltimore, again at home, in the NFL Championship game on December 29. After a scoreless first quarter against the Colts, the visitors erupted for 17 points in the second quarter on a 28-yard field goal by Lou Michaels and one- and 12-yard touchdown runs by Tom Matte. That was all the Colts needed, but they weren't done. Matte scored again in the third quarter on a two-yard touchdown run. In the fourth quarter Michaels kicked another field goal, this one from 10 yards, and Timmy Brown had a four-yard touchdown run.

Bill Nelsen was 11-of-26 for 132 yards with two interceptions. Milt Morin had three receptions for 41 yards, and Charlie Harraway had four catches for 40 yards and six rushes for 26 yards. Earl Morrall was 11-of-25 for 169 yards with a pick. Matte ran the ball 17 times for 88 yards with the three touchdowns and had two receptions for 15 yards. Jerry Hill rushed the ball 11 times for 60 yards. Willie Richardson had three receptions for 78 yards, including a 38-yarder from Morrall.

In 1969 the Browns finished 10-3-1, won the Century Division again, and for the second straight year defeated the Cowboys in the Eastern Conference title game, this time at Dallas by a resounding 38-14 score. A week later, on January 4, 1970, in the NFL Championship game they were creamed 27-7 by the Vikings in Minnesota. It was all Vikings from the start, beginning with Joe Kapp's seven-yard touchdown run and his 75-yard touchdown pass to Gene Washington that gave them a 14-0 lead after one quarter. The home team upped its lead to 24-0 at halftime on a 30-yard field goal by Fred Cox and a 20-yard touchdown run by Dave Osborn. The Minnesota lead grew to 27-0 on a 32-yard, third-quarter field goal by Cox. The Browns' only points came in the final stanza when Nelsen hit Gary Collins on a three-yard touchdown pass.

Nelsen was 17-of-33 for 181 yards with the touchdown and two interceptions. Leroy Kelly ran the ball 15 times for 80 yards and had two receptions for 17 yards. Bo Scott had five receptions for 56 yards, including a 35-yarder from Nelsen. Paul Warfield caught four passes for 47 yards, and Collins had five catches for 43 yards with the touchdown. Kapp was 7-of-13 for 169 yards with the touchdown. Osborn had 18 rushes for 108 yards with the touchdown, while Washington had three receptions for 120 yards with the touchdown.

The 1986 Browns went 12-4, won the AFC Central Division title, and, behind an incredible fourth-quarter comeback, defeated the visiting New York Jets 23-20 in double overtime in a divisional playoff. A week later in the AFC Championship game on January 11, 1987, in Cleveland, they lost 23-20 in overtime to the Denver Broncos. The Browns took a 7-0 first-quarter lead when Bernie Kosar connected with Herman Fontenot on a seven-yard touchdown pass. The score was 10-10 at halftime and 13-10 Denver entering the fourth quarter. The Browns tied it again at 13, and then Kosar found Brian Brennan on a spectacular 48-yard touchdown catch-and-run late in the game. Brennan caught Kosar's underthrown aerial at the 16-yard line, completely faked out Broncos strong safety Dennis Smith, and waltzed into the end zone. Brennan's heroics gave the Browns a 20-13 lead—and an apparent berth in Super Bowl XXI—with 5:43 to go.

That was when John Elway took control, however. With the Broncos pinned on their own two-yard line following a miscue by Gene Lang on the ensuing kickoff, the fourth-year "Browns Killer" led his team on a remarkable 98-yard touchdown drive—including a 20-yard completion to Mark Jackson on 3rd-and-18—to tie the game with 38 seconds left. The tying touchdown came when Elway fired a five-yard strike to Jackson. Elway's masterpiece, known simply as "The Drive," was the impetus for Denver's stunning victory.

Kosar was 18-of-32 for 259 yards with the two touchdowns and two interceptions and was sacked once. Kevin Mack ran the ball 26 times for 94 yards and had two receptions for 20 yards. Brennan had four receptions for 72 yards with the touchdown, while Fontenot had seven catches for 66 yards with the touchdown. Elway was 22-of-38 for 244 yards with the touchdown and a pick; he was sacked twice. He ran the ball four times for 56 yards, including a 34-yarder. Sammy Winder carried the ball 26 times for 83 yards. Steve Watson had three receptions for 55 yards, and Steve Sewell had three catches for 47 yards.

In the strike-shortened 1987 season the Browns finished 10-5, won the Central Division again, and defeated the Indianapolis Colts 38-21 in a divisional playoff game at Cleveland. A week later, on January 17, 1988, they faced the Broncos again for the AFC title—this time in Denver—and, like the year before, the Broncos won a thriller. The final was 38-33.

The first half was all Broncos as they were up 21-3 at the intermission. Kosar hit Reggie Langhorne on an 18-yard touchdown strike, but Elway connected with Jackson for an 80-yard touchdown catch-and-run down the right sideline, which looked to be the dagger to the Browns' heart as Denver took a commanding 28-10 third-quarter lead. Cleveland refused to die, though. Byner scored two touchdowns—one on a 32-yard pass from Kosar, the other on a four-yard run—to pull his team within 28-24. It was 31-24 after three quarters.

Kosar hit Webster Slaughter on a four-yard touchdown pass to tie the game at 31. Winder caught a 20-yard touchdown pass from Elway to give Denver the lead again at 38-31. With the ball on the Broncos' eight-yard line late in the game, Byner, bursting off left tackle and smelling the end zone, was stripped of the football by Jeremiah Castille at the three-yard line; Castille then fell on the ball at the three. Byner's blunder (or Castille's great defensive play) became aptly known as "The Fumble." An intentional safety by Denver accounted for the game's final points.

An exhausted Earnest Byner right after "The Fumble," January 17, 1988. (AndersonsClevelandDesign.com)

Kosar was 26-of-41 for 356 yards with the three touchdowns and an interception; he was sacked twice. Byner rushed the ball 15 times for 67 yards with the touchdown and had seven receptions for 120 yards, including a 53-yarder from Kosar, with the touchdown. Mack ran the ball 12 times for 61 yards and had four receptions for 28 yards. Slaughter had four catches for 53 yards with the touchdown. Elway was 14-of-26 for 281 yards with three touchdowns and one interception and was sacked twice. Winder rushed the ball 20 times for 72 yards and had three receptions for 34 yards with the touchdown. Lang carried the ball five times for 51 yards, including a 42-yarder, with the touchdown. Jackson had four catches for 134 yards with the touchdown, while Ricky Nattiel caught five passes for 95 yards with a touchdown.

The 1989 Browns went 9-6-1, won the Central Division, and outscored the Buffalo Bills 34-30 in a divisional playoff shootout in Cleveland. The next week, on January 14, 1990, in the AFC title game, they took on a familiar foe—the Broncos, in Denver again. They lost 37-21. Just like two years earlier, the Broncos took a big lead, 24-7 in the third quarter. And just like two years earlier, the Browns came back. Brennan caught a 10-yard touchdown pass—his second of the game—from Kosar, and Tim Manoa ran for a two-yard touchdown run as they cut the deficit to 24-21 entering the fourth quarter. Then, unlike two years before, Elway took control in the late going. He fired a 39-yard scoring strike to Winder, and then David Treadwell put the icing on the cake with two field goals.

Kosar, battling chronic elbow and hand injuries, was 19-of-44 for 210 yards with the two touchdowns and three interceptions; he was sacked four times. Mack ran the ball six times for 36 yards. Langhorne had five receptions for 78 yards, and Brennan caught five balls for 58 yards with the two touchdowns. Elway was 20-of-36 for 385 yards with three touchdowns and was sacked once. He ran the ball five times for 39 yards, including a 25-yarder. Mike Young had two receptions for 123 yards, including a 70-yard touchdown pass from Elway. Vance Johnson had seven receptions for 91 yards, and Sewell had three catches for 55 yards, including a 43-yarder from Elway.

16. d. 1972, 1973, 1974. There is quite a story behind the years leading up to those three preseason games. It was a classic case of clashing egos—Paul Brown vs. Art Modell. From Day 1 when Modell purchased majority ownership of the Browns on March 21, 1961, it was the Hatfields and McCoys, the Ewings and Barneses.

Modell had been a young advertising executive from New York City with an avid interest in professional football who had always dreamed of owning a pro football team. Brown was Cleveland's living legend of a head coach who had rebuilt tradition-steeped programs at places like Massillon Washington High School and Ohio State University before building the Cleveland franchise from scratch in 1946 into a dynasty that played in 10 straight championship games, winning seven of them, from 1946-55. The team was even named after him.

Unlike the previous ownership, Modell wanted to be involved in the day-to-day operation of the team, including player personnel decisions. This didn't exactly endear him to Brown, who was accustomed to making team-related moves himself. As the Browns were sinking to mediocrity—posting an 8-5-1 record in 1961 and a 7-6-1 mark in 1962—Modell's relationship with his head coach was deteriorating as well, and at a rapid pace.

The fact that several players' faith in Brown was crumbling, too, only worsened matters. Many of the Browns felt their coach's play-calling had become too conservative for the changing times, that the game was passing him by. Many players were also growing weary of his boot camp-like mentality, which had worked so well in the past (Brown for two years had been the head football coach and athletic officer at the Great Lakes Naval Training Center outside of Chicago).

D-Day—Dismissal Day—came on January 9, 1963, when Modell shocked the city of Cleveland, not to mention the football world, by announcing Brown's firing. As the news spread, many had difficulty fathoming what had transpired. Here was a former ad executive whose football know-how was not exactly George Halas-like. They were letting go a man whose knowledge of the game was at such a high level that he was the one who invented the facemask.

A bitter—and devastated—Brown spent the following year in Cleveland, free of grumbling players and interfering owners, then took up the quiet life at his home in La Jolla, California. Meanwhile, new head coach Blanton Collier, who had been Brown's offensive backs coach, injected a much-needed drive into the stagnant franchise and led it back to the upper echelon of the NFL. With Collier implementing a more wide-open offensive attack, the Browns won the league championship in 1964, his second year at the helm, and made three more title-game appearances in his tenure, which lasted through 1970.

With his former team busy playing in championship games, Brown returned to the game he loved. He and his family sold the city of Cincinnati on a pro football team, and the Brown family was awarded an AFL franchise on September 27, 1967, some two months after Brown had been inducted into the Pro Football Hall of Fame. Brown named his new team "Bengals" after two previous Cincinnati Bengals franchises that competed in two different AFLs in the late 1930s and early 1940s. A rivalry with his old team, not to mention a revenge factor, surely stirring in his mind, Brown outfitted the Bengals in similar attire to that of the Browns. Brown would be part-owner, general manager, and head coach.

After two years in the AFL, the Bengals joined the NFL in 1970, and were placed in the AFC Central Division with Pittsburgh, Houston, and, yes, Cleveland. In 1970 Brown's Bengals beat Modell's Browns in a preseason game at Cincinnati but then lost three of the first four regular-season meetings with them that season and the next.

The following summer, in 1972, was the first of the three exhibition games between the two teams in Columbus. The Bengals won 27-21 on September 3, but the Browns won the last two meetings—24-6 on August 19, 1973, and 21-17 on September 1, 1974. Interest in the game was rabid at first but waned dramatically. Attendance at the first game was 84,816. The mark dropped to 73,421 for the second game, and only 36,326 showed up for the last game.

17. Four. They played in the annual summer exhibition contest in Chicago in 1951, from 1955-56, and in 1965. The game was played from 1934-76 except for 1974, when it was cancelled due to an NFL players' strike. It matched a team of star college seniors from the previous season against the defending NFL champion from 1934-66

Blanton Collier (left) shakes hands with his former mentor and the man he replaced seven years earlier, Bengals head coach Paul Brown, October 11, 1970. (The Cleveland Press Collection, Michael Schwartz Library, Cleveland State University)

and the defending Super Bowl champion from 1967-76.

The game was the idea of Arch Ward, the sports editor of the *Chicago Tribune* and the driving force behind Major League

Baseball's All-Star Game. The game originally was a benefit for Chicago-area charities and was played at Soldier Field with the exception of two years, 1943 and 1944, when it was held at Northwestern University's Dyche Stadium in nearby Evanston.

The Chicago game was one of several "pro vs. rookie" college all-star games held across the United States in its early years. Other such games occurred in 1938 and 1939, but they were regional games held elsewhere and were not as high-profile as the game in Chicago. Because of this, the Chicago game survived far longer than its contemporaries.

The first Chicago College All-Star Game was played on August 31, 1934. The College All-Stars battled the hometown Bears to a scoreless tie in front of 79,432 fans. Three times—in 1942 and from 1947-48—the game attracted crowds of more than 100,000, with the 1947 contest, a 16-0 win by the College All-Stars over the Bears, drawing an all-time high of 105,840 fans. The final Chicago College All-Star Game was played on July 23, 1976. The Pittsburgh Steelers defeated the College All-Stars 24-0 before a crowd of 52,095 in a game that was called with 1:22 remaining in the third quarter due to heavy rain. Other than the two games played in Dyche Stadium, the attendance at that 1976 game was the lowest of any Chicago College All-Star Game. Enthusiasm—and attendance—for the game had begun to erode by the early 1970s.

The Browns, who had beaten the Rams, the Lions twice, and the Colts, respectively, in the previous seasons' championship games, won all four Chicago College All-Star Games they played in—33-0 in 1951, 30-27 in 1955, 26-0 in 1956, and 24-16 in 1965. A Most Valuable Player award was given from 1938-73 and was always awarded to a player on the College All-Stars. The MVP in the 1951 game was

Lewis McFadin of the University of Texas. The MVP in 1955 was quarterback Ralph Guglielmi of the University of Notre Dame. The 1956 MVP was linebacker Bob Pellegrini of the University of Maryland. The MVP in 1965 was quarterback John Huarte of the University of Notre Dame.

The All-Star Game, which raised more than $4 million for charity throughout the course of its 42-game run, was won 31 times by the pros, nine times by the All-Stars, and there were two ties.

18. d. Bob Golic. A nose tackle, Golic's first-quarter defensive gem tied the game, which was played in Milwaukee, at seven. Dickey had given the 4-5 Packers a 7-0 lead when he hit John Jefferson on an 18-yard touchdown pass. Dickey had two second-quarter touchdown passes—to Paul Coffman and Gary Lewis, respectively—to give Green Bay a 21-7 lead at the half. Another Dickey scoring strike, this one a two-yarder to Gerry Ellis, upped the home team's lead to 28-7 entering the fourth quarter. The 5-4 Browns pulled within 28-21 on a pair of Brian Sipe touchdown passes—20 yards to Bobby Jones and 19 yards to Dwight Walker. Ellis put the game away, however, when he ran 25 yards for a touchdown.

Golic had signed with the Browns via waivers on September 2, 1982. He had four sacks that year, 3.5 in 1983, two in 1984, three in 1985, and 1.5 in 1987. He left the team after the 1988 season through Plan B Free Agency. He was selected to the Pro Bowl from 1985-87.

19. Rocky Belk. A wide receiver, I was a seventh-round draft choice in 1983 out of the University of Miami. As a Hurricane, I saw little action my freshman year in 1979. As a sophomore,

I had eight receptions for 175 yards with a touchdown in help-ing Miami to a 9-3 record, upsets of Florida State and Florida, and a 20-10 victory over Virginia Tech in the Peach Bowl. In my junior year of 1981 I had 15 receptions for 451 yards with three touchdowns as we went 9-2, including another upset of Florida, another win over Florida State, and a memorable 17-14 shocker over top-ranked Penn State. As a senior, I caught a team-leading 35 passes for a team-best 645 yards, again with three touchdowns, as we finished 7-4.

My first two receptions with the Browns came on November 20, 1983, in a 30-0 victory at New England. One was a two-yard touchdown pass from Sipe, the other a 39-yarder from Sipe. A week later, on November 27, I had one reception for 23 yards in a 41-23 home win over Baltimore. Seven days later, on December 4, I had one reception for 13 yards in a 27-6 loss to the Broncos in Denver. Then came my long touchdown catch in the season-ending triumph over the Steelers. The 1983 season was my only one with the Browns.

20. b. 2002. The game was on September 8 in Cleveland. It was a wild shootout from the very start. The Chiefs led 7-6 after one quarter, and the Browns led 20-14 at halftime and then 27-17 after three quarters. The two teams had just scratched the surface, however. In the fourth quarter alone there were 35 points scored and five lead changes. After Phil Dawson's 34-yard field goal upped the Browns' lead to 30-17, Priest Holmes scored on touchdown runs of 26 and 15 yards for a 31-30 Kansas City lead. Kelly Holcomb hit Quincy Morgan on a 44-yard touchdown pass as Cleveland forged back ahead 36-31. Holmes scored again, this time from seven yards out with 3:05 to go for a 37-36 Chiefs advantage. Dawson connected on a 41-yard field goal to give the Browns a 39-37 lead with 29 seconds left.

A few moments later, on Kansas City's ensuing possession, was when things really got crazy. From the Chiefs' 47-yard line, Trent Green dropped back to pass. It looked like Rudd sacked the Chiefs' quarterback as time expired. However, Green lateraled the ball to right tackle John Tait just before he went down. Rudd did not see this and, thinking the game was over, removed his helmet and threw it in the air in celebration of what he thought was a Browns victory. Tait lumbered to the Browns' 26-yard line, where he was knocked out of bounds. That would have been the end of the game, but Rudd's premature helmet toss resulted in an unsportsmanlike conduct penalty, and a game cannot end on a defensive penalty. Thus Kansas City got to run an untimed play, and the ball was moved to the 13-yard line (half the distance to the goal line from the end of Tait's run due to the penalty). Morten Andersen then kicked a 30-yard field goal to give the Chiefs an unbelievable 40-39 victory.

Holcomb, who started in place of the injured Tim Couch, was 27-of-39 for 326 yards with three touchdowns; he was sacked once. Morgan had nine receptions for 151 yards with two touchdowns, Kevin Johnson had eight receptions for 96 yards, and Dennis Northcutt had a 43-yard touchdown catch from Holcomb. Green was 20-of-29 for 276 yards with a touchdown and a pick. Holmes rushed the ball 22 times for 122 yards with four touchdowns. Eddie Kennison had four receptions for 120 yards, including a 64-yarder from Green, while Tony Gonzalez caught five balls for 87 yards with a touchdown.

21. November 12, 2000. The Browns defeated the Patriots 19-11 that day, also in Cleveland. The 2000 season was Belichick's first year at the helm for the Patriots. They went on to finish just 5-11 with Drew Bledsoe as the quarterback and a rookie by the name of Tom Brady on the bench. The Browns entered the game with a 2-8 record and, with Tim Couch done for the year due to injury, Doug Pederson as their quarterback.

The Browns took a 3-0 first-quarter lead on Phil Dawson's 39-yard field goal. The Patriots tied the game when Adam Vinatieri booted a 38-yard field goal. In the second quarter the Browns scored on a nine-yard touchdown pass from Pederson to Aaron Shea and a 43-yard field goal by Dawson for a 13-3 halftime lead. Two more Dawson treys—35-yarders late in the third quarter and early in the fourth—upped their lead to 19-3. Bledsoe threw a two-yard touchdown pass to Rod Rutledge for the final points.

Pederson was 20-of-37 for 138 yards with the touchdown and was sacked once. Travis Prentice rushed the ball 19 times for 84 yards. Bledsoe was 21-of-35 for 212 yards with the touchdown and an interception and was sacked four times. J.R. Redmond ran the ball 10 times for 60 yards. Kevin Faulk had eight receptions for 96 yards, and Terry Glenn caught six passes for 65 yards.

The Browns' win over the Patriots a decade later came two weeks after they shocked the defending Super Bowl Champion Saints in the Superdome. The Browns took a 10-0 lead after one quarter on a 38-yard Dawson field goal and a two-yard touchdown run by Peyton Hillis. It was 17-7 at halftime and, after Colt McCoy scored on a 16-yard run, the Browns led 24-7 after three quarters. Hillis's 35-yard touchdown run with 2:38 to go was the game's final points and the icing on the cake.

McCoy was 14-of-19 for 174 yards. Hillis had 29 rushes for 184 yards with the two touchdowns and had three receptions for 36 yards. Mohamed Massaquoi had four receptions for 58 yards. Brady was 19-of-36 for 224 yards with two touchdowns and was sacked once. Danny Woodhead carried the ball nine times for 54 yards and had two receptions for 38 yards. Aaron Hernandez had five receptions for 48 yards with two touchdowns, while Rob Gronkowski had four catches for 47 yards.

22. St. Louis Cardinals. The Browns were coming off a 27-13 victory at Washington in their season opener. The Cardinals, who were Eastern Conference rivals of the Browns, had beaten Dallas 16-6 on the road in their opener the week before. The Cleveland-St. Louis game, which was played on September 20, was a wild one from the start.

The Cardinals actually led almost the entire game, including when they took a 7-0 lead in the first quarter on a 22-yard touchdown pass from Charley Johnson to John David Crow. Two Lou Groza field goals and one by Jim Bakken made the score 10-6 after one quarter. It was 13-9 when Paul Warfield caught a 40-yard touchdown pass from Frank Ryan to give the Browns a 16-13 halftime lead.

St. Louis forged ahead again on a 38-yard scoring strike from Johnson to Sonny Randle, and then a 44-yard field goal by Bakken upped its lead to 23-16. Ryan hit Gary Collins for a seven-yard touchdown pass to tie the score entering the fourth quarter. Johnson hit Randle again for a touchdown pass, this time a 50-yarder, for a seven-point Cardinals lead. The Browns came back, though, and went ahead again, 33-30, on a 25-yard field goal by Groza and a one-yard touchdown run by

Jim Brown. Bakken connected on a 28-yard field goal for the game's final points.

Ryan was 12-of-26 for 189 yards with the two touchdowns and two interceptions. Brown rushed the ball 21 times for 79 yards with the touchdown. Collins had six receptions for 105 yards with the touchdown, and Warfield had three catches for 63 yards with the touchdown. Johnson was 14-of-27 for 241 yards with the three touchdowns and a pick. Crow had 11 rushes for 58 yards and three receptions for 29 yards with the touchdown. Joe Childress had 14 carries for 52 yards and three receptions for 50 yards. Randle caught four passes for 121 yards with the two touchdowns.

23. Bo Scott. I was a third-round draft pick in 1965 out of Ohio State University. Because the Browns' backfield was already full of quality backs such as future Hall of Famers Jim Brown and Leroy Kelly, as well as Ernie Green, I elected to sign with the CFL's Ottawa Rough Riders. I was an All-Star and helped my team to the 1968 Grey Cup championship.

I joined the Browns in 1969. I was used mainly as a kickoff returner that year and had both a team-leading 25 returns and 722 return yards (including a 65-yarder), which led the league. In our 38-14 rout of the Cowboys in the Eastern Conference championship game, I had 11 rushes for 33 yards, including a pair of two-yard touchdown runs, and had two receptions for 39 yards. A week later in our 27-7 loss at Minnesota in the NFL title game, I caught five passes for 56 yards.

In a Week 8 loss at Oakland during that pretty decent 1970 season I had, I had 14 carries for 101 yards, including a 63-yard touchdown run, and had two receptions for 20 yards. The next season I had 179 rushes for 606 yards with nine touchdowns and 30 receptions for 233 yards with a touchdown. In a 27-24 comeback win at Cincinnati on October 17 I ran the ball 14 times for 42 yards, including two short touchdowns, and had a seven-yard touchdown catch, too. In our 20-3 divisional playoff defeat at home to the Colts, I had five receptions for 41 yards.

In 1972 I ran the ball 123 times for 571 yards with two touchdowns and caught 23 passes for 172 yards. Included was a 27-10 victory over Buffalo on November 26 in which I had eight carries for 40 yards and six catches for 62 yards. In our 20-14 divisional playoff loss at Miami on Christmas Eve, I rushed the ball 16 times for 94 yards and had four receptions for 30 yards. I was mainly a backup in both 1973 and 1974 and was waived on August 8, 1975.

Joe Jones (left) and John Garlington chase Dallas's Bob Hayes in the end zone for a safety, the Browns' only score in a 6-2 defeat, December 12, 1970. (The Cleveland Press Collection, Michael Schwartz Library, Cleveland State University)

24. c. Three. They finished 7-7 in 1970, 8-8 in 1978, and 8-8 in 1985. The 1970 Browns began the new decade with a bang by beating Joe Namath and the New York Jets 31-21 in the first ABC *Monday Night Football* game on September 21 before 85,703 fans, the most ever for a Browns home game. Homer Jones returned the second half kickoff 94 yards for a touchdown. Billy

Andrews put the nail in New York's coffin when he made a diving interception of a Namath pass, got up, and returned it 25 yards for a touchdown with 35 seconds left.

The Browns were a model of inconsistency, but due to their division rivals' lackluster play as well, remained in the AFC Central title hunt. They lost out on the division championship on the final day of the season when the Cincinnati Bengals, after a 1-6 start, won their seventh straight game to finish 8-6, a game ahead of the Browns, whose victory in Denver later that day, as a result, was meaningless.

The 1978 Browns got off to the franchise's first 3-0 start in 15 years, including an overtime win at home against the Bengals and a heart stopper against the Falcons in Atlanta. They easily could have been 5-0 if not for two highly disputed officiating calls that led to stinging defeats to Pittsburgh and Houston. The team rebounded by beating the Saints in the Superdome to improve to 4-2. Four losses in the next five games, however, pretty much doomed the Browns before wins over Baltimore and Los Angeles renewed slim playoff hopes. A 47-24 drubbing at the hands of the Seahawks in the Kingdome on December 3 ended any realistic postseason aspirations.

The 1985 Browns split their first four games. Rookie Bernie Kosar saw his first action in Week 5 at home against New England when Gary Danielson injured his right shoulder in the second quarter. Although Kosar fumbled his first snap, he completed his first seven passes as the Browns used a late goal-line stand to defeat the Patriots 24-20, leaving the team alone atop the Central Division for the first time in two years.

Kosar's first start was a winning one as he connected with Clarence Weathers for a 68-yard touchdown pass in a 21-6 triumph over the Oilers the next week in the Astrodome, upping

Cleveland's record to 4-2. With Danielson still out and Kosar the starter, the Browns lost their next four games to drop to 4-6 and a tie with Houston for last place. But with the Central Division experiencing another down year overall, the Browns were far from out of the race. They got back on track by beating Buffalo 17-7 at home. Danielson was back as the starter the next week at home against Cincinnati. The veteran directed the Browns to a key win when, early in the third quarter, he beat a blitz and hooked up with Weathers on a perfect 72-yard touchdown strike—the Browns' only pass of the entire second half—that virtually sealed a 24-6 victory.

The Browns dodged a bullet the next week against the Giants in New York, winning a 35-33 thriller when Eric Schubert missed a 34-yard field goal as time expired. Danielson, aching arm and all, came off the bench to lead two late touchdown drives, but he was done for the year when he re-aggravated his shoulder on a harmless swing pass to Kevin Mack on the winning drive. It was up to Kosar to lead the Browns to their first postseason berth in three years. He produced just one victory—a 28-21 triumph over Houston—in the final three games, but it was enough for the team to sneak into the playoffs as Central Division champs.

Although they finished with only a .500 record, the Browns received a first-round bye because they won their division. They were heavy underdogs in their divisional playoff matchup with the Dan Marino-led Dolphins in Miami. Earnest Byner's relentless effort sparked Cleveland, though, and when he scored his second touchdown of the day on a 66-yard run early in the third quarter, the Browns found themselves ahead 21-3. One of the most stunning upsets in NFL playoff history went up in flames, however, as the Dolphins recovered to pull out a 24-21 win.

25. Thom Darden. Darden had 45 interceptions in his career that lasted from 1972-74 and 1976-81. He was a first-round draft choice in 1972 from the University of Michigan. As a strong safety in his rookie season that year, he tied for the team lead with three interceptions and recovered a fumble for a club that finished 10-4 and qualified for the playoffs. He also returned 15 punts for 61 yards, including a 37-yarder in a Week 4 loss to Kansas City. He returned a punt 38 yards in the Browns' divisional playoff loss at Miami.

In 1973 Darden switched to free safety, where he would remain for the rest of his career. He picked off one pass, thrown by Norm Snead, which he returned 36 yards in a Week 3 win over the New York Giants. He also had a fumble recovery and returned nine punts for 51 yards. The next season he had a team-leading eight interceptions, including two in a game twice—in a Week 4 loss to the Raiders and a Week 9 win over the Patriots, the latter in which he also returned a fumble 29 yards for a touchdown. He had 21 punt returns for 173 yards, too. He missed the 1975 season due to preseason knee surgery.

Darden had a team-best seven interceptions and a fumble recovery in 1976, including two in a season-opening 38-17 rout of the New York Jets. In 1977 he intercepted a team-high six passes, including one he returned 18 yards for a touchdown in a 44-7 rout of the Chiefs on October 30. In his lone Pro Bowl year of 1978 his 10 picks led the entire NFL and tie him with Tom Colella (1946) and Anthony Henry (2001) for the Browns' all-time single-season record. He had three games—at Atlanta, at Pittsburgh, and at home against Buffalo—in which he intercepted two passes. He also returned one 42 yards against the 49ers in the season opener. He had two fumble recoveries, as well.

Thom Darden reaches for, and knocks down, a pass intended for Lynn Swann in the Cleveland end zone during an 18-16 upset of the Steelers, October 10, 1976. (AndersonsClevelandDesign.com)

Darden had a team-leading five interceptions in 1979, including one off Roger Staubach that he returned 39 yards for a touchdown in a 26-7 upset of the Dallas Cowboys on Monday Night Football. He had a fumble recovery that year, too. Darden added two picks in 1980 and three in 1981, the latter in which he also recovered two fumbles.

HALL OF FAME LEVEL

To get these 25 questions correct, you must be a Browns history guru. Good luck! You'll need it.

1. Who was the first first-round selection by the Browns in a regular draft who actually played for the team? *Answer on page 146.*

2. Leroy Kelly led the Browns in rushing yards every season from 1966-72. Greg Pruitt was the team's leading ground gainer every season from 1974-78. Who was the rushing leader the season in between, 1973? *Answer on page 147.*

3. In which of the following college towns have the Browns not played a preseason game? *Answer on page 148.*
   a. Ann Arbor, Michigan
   b. Stillwater, Oklahoma
   c. Austin, Texas
   d. Lincoln, Nebraska

4. Otto Graham was not the starting quarterback in the Browns' first game ever on September 6, 1946, at home against the Miami Seahawks. Who was? *Answer on page 151.*

5. How many regular-season games have the Browns played in January? *Answer on page 152.*

a. Three   b. Five

c. Seven   d. Nine

6. Against what team did the Browns squander a 14-point lead with less than a minute to go, only to lose in heartbreaking fashion on November 4, 2001? *Answer on page 155.*

7. In their "replacement" games during the 1987 players' strike, the Browns won at New England on October 4, lost at home to Houston on October 11, and won at Cincinnati on October 18. What were the scores of those games, respectively? *Answer on page 156.*

a. 20-0, 16-10, 34-0

b. 20-10, 15-10, 34-0

c. 20-10, 17-10, 34-3

d. 20-0, 13-10, 34-3

8. How many Heisman Trophy winners have played for the Browns? *Answer on page 158.*

a. Three   b. Five

c. Seven   d. Nine

9. Josh Gordon set an NFL record in 2013 for most receiving yards in a four-game stretch with _____ from November 17 to December 8. *Answer on page 161.*

a. 574   b. 674

c. 774   d. 874

10. Had the Browns not blown a 17-point, third-quarter lead in their 36-33 AFC Wild Card Playoff loss at Pittsburgh on January 5, 2003, which team would they have played the next week in the divisional playoffs? *Answer on page 162.*

11. When was the last time the Browns won a playoff game on the road? *Answer on page 163.*
    a. December 24, 1967   b. December 29, 1968
    c. December 28, 1969   d. January 4, 1970

12. The Browns have played on Thanksgiving Day five times. True or false? *Answer on page 164.*

13. Clay Matthews and Ozzie Newsome were the first two players drafted by the Browns in 1978. I was the third player chosen that year. Who am I? *Answer on page 167.*

14. What was the only season the Browns drew at least 80,000 fans for every home game? *Answer on page 167.*
    a. 1950   b. 1964
    c. 1969   d. 1980

15. The 1984 Browns finished with just a 5-11 record, but they were competitive in, and had a chance to win, nine of their losses. In fact, eight of their defeats came by four points or less. To which two teams did the Browns lose convincingly that season? *Answer on page 168.*
    a. St. Louis, San Francisco
    b. Seattle, San Francisco
    c. Seattle, San Diego
    d. San Diego, St. Louis

16. How many Browns Hall of Famers are there? *Answer on page 170.*
    a. 12   b. 14
    c. 16   d. 18

17. Match the quarterback on the left with the team against which he made his first start on the right. *Answer on page 177.*

Paul McDonald	Houston Oilers
Mike Phipps	San Diego Chargers
Brian Sipe	Pittsburgh Steelers
Bernie Kosar	Cincinnati Bengals

18. Ricky Feacher, who had signed as a free agent early in the 1976 season, was a backup wide receiver in 1980 but came to the rescue with two crucial touchdown catches on December 21 that year in a season-ending 27-24 victory over the Bengals in Cincinnati that gave Cleveland the AFC Central Division title. Which team chose him in the 10th round of the 1976 draft? *Answer on page 180.*

19. Since the NFL adopted overtime for regular-season games in 1974, the Browns have had two games end in a tie. True or false? *Answer on page 181.*

20. Although they finished 10-4 in 1963, that year was a tragic one for the Browns. Three players, including 1961 Heisman Trophy winner Ernie Davis, died before training camp even began. Who were the other two? *Answer on page 182.*

21. The Browns have played two Tuesday-night games—one in Miami and one in Baltimore. In which seasons did they occur? *Answer on page 183.*

22. The Browns have been featured on the cover of *Sports Illustrated* _____ times. *Answer on page 184.*

    a. 11   b. 13

    c. 15   d. 17

23. Which player has the distinction of having scored the NFL's first-ever two-point conversion? *Answer on page 184.*

24. _____ players have won Rookie-of-the-Year awards as a Brown. *Answer on page 185.*

    a. Two   b. Three

    c. Four   d. Five

25. Match the quarterbacks and seasons on the left with the number of touchdown passes on the right. *Answer on page 188.*

Brian Sipe, 1983	23
Bill Nelsen, 1969	29
Bernie Kosar, 1986	26
Derek Anderson, 2007	17

HALL OF FAME
LEVEL – ANSWERS

1. Ken Carpenter. A halfback, Carpenter was chosen out of Oregon State University with the 13th overall pick of the 1950 NFL Draft. For a Browns team that won the NFL Championship in 1950, he rushed the ball 35 times for 181 yards with a touchdown and had five receptions for 45 yards. He also had five kickoff returns for 98 yards and four punt returns for 58 yards. Carpenter's best game of the year was a 31-0 victory over the Colts at Baltimore on September 24 in which he had three carries for 100 yards, including a 61-yard touchdown—his only score of the season—in the fourth quarter. In Cleveland's 30-28 victory over the Los Angeles Rams in the NFL title game, he returned three kickoffs for 58 yards.

In 1951, Carpenter's only Pro Bowl year, he ran the ball 85 times for 402 yards with four touchdowns and had 12 receptions for 183 yards with two touchdowns. He returned nine kickoffs for 196 yards and 14 punts for 173 yards, all team highs (he was co-leader in punt returns). In a Week 2 win at Los Angeles he scored three touchdowns in a row—on a 45-yard pass from Otto Graham in the first quarter and on two- and seven-yard runs in the third quarter. A month later in a 34-17 victory over the Chicago Cardinals, he rushed for 118 yards on 18 carries and had three catches for 49 yards. In a 24-17 loss to the Rams at Los Angeles in the NFL Championship game, he again caught three balls for 49 yards, including a two-yard touchdown run that tied the game in the fourth quarter. He also had five kickoff returns for 132 yards.

The next season Carpenter rushed the ball 72 times for 408 yards with three touchdowns and had 16 receptions for 136 yards with a touchdown. He had a team-leading 11 kickoff returns for a team-best 234 yards and 10 punt returns for 139 yards, including a 54-yarder for a touchdown in a 48-24 win at Washington on November 30. His best game of the season was a 37-7 triumph over the Rams in the opener in which he ran the ball 16 times for 145 yards and had three receptions for 54 yards, including a 41-yarder for a touchdown from Graham. In 1953 he had 46 carries for 195 yards with three touchdowns and nine receptions for 109 yards with two touchdowns. He also had both a team-leading 16 kickoff returns and 367 kickoff return yards. He left after the season to play in the CFL.

2. Ken Brown. Brown, who never played in college, was a running back. He was mainly a backup in his first three seasons, the latter, 1972, in which he rushed the ball 32 times for 114 yards with two touchdowns and had five receptions for 64 yards. In 1973 he ran the ball a team-leading 161 times for 537 yards and caught 22 passes for 187 yards. Included was a 26-rush, 93-yard performance in a 17-10 victory over the visiting Bengals on October 7. The next week in a Monday night loss to the Dolphins he ran the ball 17 times for 55 yards and had three receptions for 30 yards. Six days later, on October 21, he gained 61 yards on 14 carries in a 42-13 home rout of the Oilers. A month later, in a 7-3 win at Oakland, he had 23 rushes for 82 yards. In a crucial victory over the visiting Steelers on November 25, he caught a 46-yard pass—his only reception of the game—from Mike Phipps.

In 1974 Brown had 125 rushes for 458 yards with four touchdowns and 29 receptions for 194 yards with two touchdowns. Included was a 12-carry, 78-yard performance in a season-opening 33-7 loss to the Bengals at Cincinnati. In a 15-10 defeat to Buffalo on November 24 he ran the ball 15 times for 73 yards and had three catches for 21 yards, including a short touchdown pass from Phipps. He returned to backup status the next season.

Brown was also a kickoff returner. In 1971 he had both a team-leading 15 returns and 330 return yards, including a 35-yarder. The next year he had both a team-high 20 returns and 473 return yards, including a 47-yarder. He returned seven kickoffs for 126 yards in his final season of 1975.

3. c. Austin, Texas. The Browns defeated the Detroit Lions 34-7 on August 20, 1972, at Michigan Stadium in Ann Arbor. They lost 21-0 to the Baltimore Colts on July 31, 1976, at Memorial Stadium in Lincoln. They beat the Atlanta Falcons 31-7 on August 7, 1976, at Lewis Field in Stillwater.

The Browns have played preseason games in several other college towns and at other neutral sites through the years. In all, they have played 50 preseason games at neutral sites. Their record is 32-18. The following are the other 47 neutral-site games they have played:

*Browns 35, Brooklyn 20 (August 30, 1946, at the Rubber Bowl in Akron)

*Browns 28, Baltimore 0 (August 29, 1947, at the Rubber Bowl in Akron)

*Browns 35, Buffalo 21 (August 22, 1948, at the Rubber Bowl in Akron)

*Baltimore 21, Browns 17 (August 27, 1948, at Scott High School Stadium in Toledo)

*Browns 21, Chicago 0 (August 14, 1949, at the Glass Bowl in Toledo)

*Browns 28, Brooklyn-New York 21 (August 26, 1949, at the Rubber Bowl in Akron)

*Browns 38, Green Bay 7 (August 12, 1950, at the Glass Bowl in Toledo)

*Browns 34, Baltimore 7 (August 19, 1950, at Nippert Stadium in Cincinnati)

*Browns 35, Detroit 14 (August 25, 1950, at the Rubber Bowl in Akron)

*Browns 41, Pittsburgh 31 (September 4, 1950, at War Memorial Stadium in Buffalo)

*Browns 52, New York Yanks 0 (August 25, 1951, at the Rubber Bowl in Akron)

*Detroit 28, Browns 21 (September 6, 1952, at Archbold Stadium in Syracuse, New York)

*San Francisco 35, Browns 31 (September 13, 1952, at the Rubber Bowl in Akron)

*Browns 23, Baltimore 21 (September 7, 1953, at the Rubber Bowl in Akron)

*Detroit 56, Browns 31 (September 10, 1954, at the Cotton Bowl in Dallas)

*Browns 13, Green Bay 7 (August 20, 1955, at the Rubber Bowl in Akron)

*Detroit 31, Browns 14 (September 15, 1956, at the Rubber Bowl in Akron)

*Browns 28, Pittsburgh 13 (August 24, 1957, at the Rubber Bowl in Akron)

*Browns 10, Pittsburgh 0 (August 16, 1958, at the Rubber Bowl in Akron)

*Detroit 9, Browns 3 (August 22, 1959, at the Rubber Bowl in Akron)

*Browns 26, San Francisco 24 (September 3, 1960, at Multnomah Stadium in Portland, Oregon)

*Browns 16, Chicago 10 (September 10, 1960, at the Rubber Bowl in Akron)

*Browns 38, Pittsburgh 6 (September 2, 1961, at the Rubber Bowl in Akron)

*Browns 34, San Francisco 27 (August 25, 1962, at Multnomah Stadium in Portland, Oregon)

*Pittsburgh 16, Browns 7 (September 8, 1963, at Fawcett Stadium in Canton)

*Browns 42, Pittsburgh 7 (August 22, 1964, at the Rubber Bowl in Akron)

*Browns 28, Pittsburgh 16 (September 11, 1965, at the Rubber Bowl in Akron)

*Browns 13, Pittsburgh 10 (September 3, 1966, at Legion Field in Birmingham, Alabama)

*Philadelphia 28, Browns 13 (August 5, 1967, at Fawcett Stadium in Canton)

*Browns 24, San Francisco 19 (August 10, 1969, at Husky Stadium in Seattle)

*Minnesota 23, Browns 16 (September 13, 1969, at the Rubber Bowl in Akron)

*Browns 17, San Francisco 10 (August 15, 1970, at Tampa Stadium in Tampa)

*Kansas City 16, Browns 13 (August 22, 1970, at the Liberty Bowl in Memphis, Tennessee)

*Chicago 20, Browns 19 (August 28, 1971, at Notre Dame Stadium in South Bend, Indiana)

*Cincinnati 27, Browns 21 (September 3, 1972, at Ohio Stadium in Columbus)

*Browns 24, Cincinnati 6 (August 19, 1973, at Ohio Stadium in Columbus)

*Browns 20, Atlanta 17 (August 25, 1973, at Neyland Stadium in Knoxville, Tennessee)

*New York Giants 21, Browns 10 (September 8, 1973, at the Rubber Bowl in Akron)

*Baltimore 37, Browns 3 (August 17, 1974, at Tampa Stadium in Tampa)

*Browns 21, Cincinnati 17 (September 1, 1974, at Ohio Stadium in Columbus)

*Browns 24, New York Giants 20 (September 7, 1975, at Husky Stadium in Seattle)

*Browns 24, Atlanta 10 (August 1, 1981, at Fawcett Stadium in Canton)

*New York Jets 11, Browns 7 (August 18, 1988, at Olympic Stadium in Montreal)

*Philadelphia 17, Browns 13 (August 6, 1989, at Wembley Stadium in London)

*Chicago 13, Browns 0 (August 4, 1990, at Fawcett Stadium in Canton)

*Browns 12, New England 9 (August 14, 1993, at Sky-Dome in Toronto)

*Browns 20, Dallas 17 (OT) (August 9, 1999, at Fawcett Stadium in Canton)

4. Cliff Lewis. Lewis gave the Browns a 7-0 first-quarter lead when he threw a 19-yard touchdown pass to Mac Speedie. He was soon replaced by Graham, who wound up leading the

Browns to a 44-0 triumph. Lewis went on to be a backup to Graham for six seasons.

Lewis enjoyed most of his success as a defensive back. He signed as a free agent in 1946. He intercepted five passes that year, four in 1947, a team-leading nine in 1948, and a team-high six in 1949. He picked off one pass in 1950 and five, which tied for the team lead, in 1951. He totaled 30 picks overall.

Also a punt and kickoff returner, Lewis returned eight punts for 133 yards in 1946 and seven for 84 yards in 1947. In 1948 he had 26 punt returns for 258 yards and 20 punt returns for 174 yards the next year. On kickoff returns, he had three for 70 yards in 1946, four for 71 yards in 1947, and seven for 147 yards in 1948. Overall, he had 77 punt returns for 710 yards and 14 kickoff returns for 288 yards. He retired after the 1951 season.

5. d. Nine. They were all season finales. The first game was a 37-21 loss to the Steelers in Pittsburgh on January 2, 1983. Under the expanded postseason format due to the 1982 players' strike, the Browns, who entered 4-4, could breathe easy in that they knew that, even if they lost, the only way they would miss the playoffs was if Buffalo and New England played to a tie the same day.

The 5-3 Steelers took a 7-0 first-quarter lead when Terry Bradshaw threw a three-yard touchdown pass to Ray Pinney. The Browns tied the game in the second quarter on a short touchdown pass from Paul McDonald to Ricky Feacher. John Rodgers returned a blocked punt 18 yards for a touchdown to give Pittsburgh a 13-7 halftime lead. By the fourth quarter, the Steelers had increased their lead to 27-7. Touchdown passes from McDonald to Dave Logan and Feacher again cut the Browns' deficit to 27-21, but that is as close as they got.

The Patriots wound up beating the Bills, though, clinching a playoff berth for the Browns.

The second game was a 16-9 defeat to the Steelers in Pittsburgh on January 2, 1994. The Browns came in 7-8, the Steelers 8-7. It was pretty much a battle of field goals. Gary Anderson kicked a 36-yarder to give Pittsburgh a 3-0 second-quarter lead. Matt Stover responded with 36-, 47-, and 44-yard field goals to give the Browns a 9-3 halftime lead. Anderson connected from 38 yards to cut Cleveland's lead to 9-6 entering the fourth quarter. Neil O'Donnell hit Eric Green on a 14-yard touchdown pass as the Steelers regained the lead at 13-9. Anderson knocked home a 26-yard field goal for the game's final points.

The third game was a 22-14 victory over the Texans on January 2, 2005, in Houston. The Browns, who entered 3-12, took a 3-0 first-quarter lead on a 45-yard Phil Dawson field goal. David Carr threw a six-yard touchdown pass to Jonathan Wells to give the Texans, who came in 7-8, a 7-3 lead after the first quarter. Two Dawson field goals—from 22 and 29 yards—put the Browns up 9-7 at the half. Kelly Holcomb's nine-yard touchdown pass to Steve Heiden upped Cleveland's lead to 16-7 after three quarters. Two more Dawson field goals—from 45 and 22 yards, respectively—made it 22-7. Domanick Williams's short touchdown run late in the game was too little, too late.

The fourth game was a 20-16 home win over Baltimore on January 1, 2006. After a scoreless first quarter, the Ravens, who entered 6-9, took a 13-0 second-quarter lead on two field goals by Stover, who had followed the original Browns to Baltimore in 1996, and a nine-yard fumble return by Adalius Thomas. The Browns, who came in 5-10, responded with a pair of Dawson field goals to cut their deficit to 13-6 at the half. Stover kicked a 31-yard field goal in the third quarter to increase Baltimore's lead to 16-6. Soon after, Charlie Frye hit Antonio Bryant on a six-yard touchdown pass to pull the Browns within 16-13. The winning score came about a minute-and-a-half later when Dennis Northcutt returned a Dave Zastudil punt 62 yards for a touchdown.

The fifth game was a 23-17 triumph over the visiting Jaguars, who were 7-8 coming in, on January 3, 2010. The Browns, who entered 4-11 but on a three-game winning streak, took a 3-0 first-quarter lead on a 27-yard field goal by Dawson. A 47-yard field goal by Josh Scobee tied the game at three entering the second quarter. A 14-yard touchdown run by Josh Cribbs and another Dawson field goal gave the Browns a 13-3 half-time lead. Jerome Harrison's six-yard touchdown run upped their lead to 20-3 after three quarters. In the fourth quarter, a 33-yard Dawson field goal was sandwiched between two David Garrard touchdown passes to Zach Miller, a six-yarder and a 15-yarder, the latter of which was the final points of the game.

The sixth game was a 41-9 defeat to Pittsburgh on January 2, 2011, at Cleveland, which brought a 5-10 record into the game. It was all Steelers, who entered 11-4, from the start. Forty-three seconds into the game they took a 7-0 lead on a 56-yard touchdown pass from Ben Roethlisberger to Mike Wallace. Some seven minutes later Rashard Mendenhall's one-yard touchdown run gave Pittsburgh a 14-0 lead entering the second quarter. By halftime, the Steelers were up 31-3. They coasted the rest of the way.

The seventh game was a 13-9 loss to Pittsburgh, which entered 11-4, on January 1, 2012, in Cleveland. The 4-11 Browns took a 6-0 lead on a pair of second-quarter field goals, from 26 and 45 yards, by Dawson. Shaun Suisham's 19-yard field goal at the end of the quarter cut the Browns' lead to 6-3. Suisham's 29-yard field goal early in the third quarter made it 6-6. Some four minutes later Isaac Redman ran for a seven-yard touchdown to put Pittsburgh on top 13-6. Dawson kicked a 49-yard field goal later in the third for the game's final points.

The eighth game was a 28-12 defeat to the Steelers on January 3, 2016, in Cleveland. Pittsburgh, which entered 9-6, took a 7-0 first-quarter lead on a short touchdown pass from Roethlisberger to Heath Miller. The 3-12 Browns made it 7-3 later in the quarter on a 29-yard field goal by Travis Coons. Two second-quarter field goals by Coons sandwiched a 17-yard touchdown pass from Roethlisberger to Antonio Brown for a 14-9 Steelers halftime lead. Pittsburgh was up 17-12 early in the fourth quarter when Roethlisberger hooked up with Markus Wheaton on an eight-yard touchdown pass to make it 25-12. Chris Boswell's 21-yard field goal midway through the fourth put the game away.

The ninth game was a 27-24 overtime loss to the Steelers on January 1, 2017, at Pittsburgh. The Steelers, who entered 10-5 and their playoff seeding already set, sat some of their regulars, including Roethlisberger, Brown, and Le'Veon Bell. Still, the Browns, who came in just 1-14, squandered an early 14-0 lead. Cody Parkey's 34-yard field goal 7:17 into the extra period gave them a 24-21 lead. Pittsburgh won the game some four minutes later when Landry Jones hit Cobi Hamilton on a 26-yard touchdown pass.

6. Chicago Bears. The Browns lost 27-21 in overtime at Soldier Field in a game that the Browns were leading 21-7 with some 40 seconds left. The Browns, who entered 4-2, took a 7-0 lead 55 seconds into the game when Courtney Brown returned a fumble 25 yards for a touchdown. The Bears, who came in 5-1, tied the game with 20 seconds remaining in the first half on a two-yard touchdown run by Anthony Thomas. The Browns took a 14-7 lead early in the third quarter when Mike Sellers caught a three-yard touchdown pass from Tim Couch. They upped their lead to 21-7 late in the third on a 55-yard touchdown pass from Couch to Kevin Johnson.

The score stayed that way until late in the fourth quarter when the Bears cut their deficit to 21-14 with 28 seconds to go on a nine-yard touchdown pass from Shane Matthews to Marty Booker. Then they recovered an onside kick at the Browns' 47-yard line with 24 seconds left. Three plays later Chicago tied the score when Matthews completed a 34-yard Hail Mary pass tipped by Percy Ellsworth to James Allen with 0:00 on the clock. The Bears were to punt on the first possession of sudden death. Then, on 2nd-and-15 from the Browns' 23-yard-line, Mike Brown intercepted a pass by Couch that was batted by teammate Bryan Robinson and returned it 16 yards for the winning touchdown.

Couch was 14-of-23 for 211 yards with the two touchdowns and the one interception; he was sacked three times. James Jackson rushed the ball 22 times for 71 yards, and Johnson had five receptions for 99 yards with the touchdown. Matthews was 30-of-50 for 357 yards with the two touchdowns and three picks; he was sacked five times. Thomas had 31 rushes for 96 yards with the touchdown and had six receptions for 71 yards. Dez White had seven receptions for 92 yards, including a 32-yarder from Matthews. Booker had seven catches for 85 yards with the touchdown, while Allen caught five passes for 65 yards with the touchdown.

7. b. 20-10, 15-10, 34-0. The Browns had split their first two games, losing at New Orleans on September 13 and beating

Pittsburgh at home on September 20 (all Week 3 games were cancelled), heading into the contest against New England. After a scoreless first quarter in front of only 14,830 fans, the Patriots took a 10-0 halftime lead on a 23-yard field goal by Eric Schubert and a six-yard touchdown pass from Bob Bleier to Larry Linne. The Browns cut it to 10-6 after three quarters on two short field goals by Brian Franco. Two one-yard touchdown runs by Larry Mason were the game's final points.

Jeff Christensen was 10-of-30 for 135 yards and was sacked once. Mason rushed the ball 32 times for 133 yards with the two touchdowns. Perry Kemp had two receptions for 58 yards, including a 31-yarder from Christensen, and Derek Tennell caught three passes for 39 yards. Bleier was 10-of-26 for 138 yards with the touchdown and was sacked three times. Wayne Coffey had three receptions for 66 yards, including a 35-yarder from Bleier. Linne had four catches for 45 yards with the touchdown.

The game against Houston drew just 38,927 fans. The Browns took a 3-0 first-quarter lead on Franco's 26-yard field goal. The Oilers forged ahead 7-3 at halftime on a 15-yard second-quarter touchdown pass from Brent Pease to Keith McDonald. They upped their lead to 13-3 entering the fourth quarter when John Diettrich connected on 45- and 23-yard field goals. The Browns pulled within a field goal when Mason caught a five-yard touchdown pass from Christensen. Jesse Baker was responsible for the game's final points when he sacked Christensen in the end zone for a safety.

Christensen was 13-of-27 for 152 yards with the touchdown and three interceptions; he was sacked four times. Kemp had five receptions for 96 yards, including a 34-yarder from Christensen. Pease was 13-of-25 for 150 yards with the touchdown and two picks and was sacked once. Herman Hunter had

28 rushes for 121 yards, and Leonard Harris caught six passes for 104 yards, including a 39-yarder from Pease.

The Browns got some much-needed help for the game against Cincinnati in the form of a handful of selected regular team members, including Ozzie Newsome, Brian Brennan, and Gary Danielson, returning to action. Before only 40,179 fans, Danielson's six-yard touchdown pass to Brennan gave them a 7-0 first-quarter lead. In the second quarter Danielson sandwiched touchdown passes to Tennell and Kemp around a 45-yard Jeff Jaeger field goal for a 24-0 lead at halftime. The Browns nailed the coffin door shut on the Bengals with a 33-yard Jaeger field goal in the third quarter and another Danielson-to-Kemp touchdown pass, a 19-yarder in the fourth quarter for the game's final points.

The Browns dominated the Bengals 29-6 in first downs, 291-40 in passing yards, 410-95 in total yards, and 42:12 to 17:48 in time of possession. Danielson was 25-of-31 for 281 yards with the four touchdowns; he was sacked twice. Mason ran the ball 20 times for 69 yards. Brennan had 10 receptions for 139 yards with the touchdown, while Kemp had five catches for 70 yards with the two touchdowns. The Browns' exceptional performance gave them a 3-2 record as the rest of the regulars returned eight nights later for an October 26 *Monday Night Football* game at home against the Los Angeles Rams.

8. c. Seven. They are Les Horvath, Howard Cassady, Charles White, Vinny Testaverde, Ty Detmer, Robert Griffin III, and Johnny Manziel. Horvath won the 1944 Heisman Trophy as a halfback and quarterback at Ohio State University. After spending 1947 and 1948 with the Los Angeles Rams, he signed as a free agent in 1949 as a defensive player and running back.

He saw little action on offense that year but did score two touchdowns. Defensively, he had two interceptions and returned a fumble 84 yards for a touchdown in a 14-3 victory over the New York Yankees in Week 3. He retired after the season.

Cassady won the 1955 Heisman Trophy as a halfback, also at Ohio State University. After six seasons with the Detroit Lions, he joined the Browns in 1962. His main activity that year came as a kickoff returner and punt returner. He returned 10 kickoffs for 233 yards and seven punts for 47 yards. He left the Browns about midway through the schedule and spent the rest of the season with the Eagles.

White won the Heisman Trophy in 1979 as a running back at the University of Southern California. He was a first-round draft choice in 1980. He was a running back from 1980-82 and in 1984. He missed the 1983 season due to a broken ankle suffered in the second preseason game. Although he scored six touchdowns his rookie year, his best season was 1981 when he rushed the ball 97 times for 342 yards with a touchdown, had 27 receptions for 219 yards, and returned 12 kickoffs for 243 yards. He was released before the start of the 1985 season.

Testaverde won the Heisman Trophy in 1986 as a quarterback at the University of Miami. He was signed as a free agent on March 31, 1993. After taking over the starting quarterback job from Bernie Kosar in Game 6 of the 1993 season, he got injured the very next week against Pittsburgh. Kosar was released two weeks later, and Testaverde returned to action in early December to finish out the season. The next year he completed 207 of 376 passes for 2,575 yards with 16 touchdowns and 18 interceptions in helping the Browns to a playoff berth and a victory over New England in the first round. He was benched midway through the 1995 season despite leading the AFC in passing but eventually won the starting job back that same year. He followed the Browns to Baltimore when the team relocated there the next season.

Detmer won the Heisman Trophy in 1990 as a quarter-back at Brigham Young University. He was traded from San Francisco on February 26, 1999, to mentor rookie Tim Couch. Detmer started the first game of the 1999 season, then served as backup until Couch sprained his foot in Week 15. He started the final game of the 1999 season. That year he completed 47 of 91 passes for 548 yards with four touchdowns and two interceptions. He injured his right Achilles and missed the entire 2000 season. He was traded to Detroit on September 2, 2001.

Griffin won the Heisman Trophy in 2011 as a quarterback at Baylor University. He was signed as a free agent on March 24, 2016. He was placed on injured reserve the day after suffering a shoulder injury as the starter in the Browns' season-opening loss to the Philadelphia Eagles. He returned to action late in the season and started the last four games. That year he completed 87 of 147 passes for 886 yards with two touchdowns and three interceptions. He also rushed the ball 31 times for 190 yards with two touchdowns. He was released on March 10, 2017.

Manziel won the Heisman Trophy in 2012 as a quarter-back at Texas A&M University. "Johnny Football," as he was known, was chosen in the first round of the 2014 draft. He waited patiently on the bench as a rookie that year behind starter Brian Hoyer, who led the Browns to a 7-4 start but struggled as the team lost two straight games with their playoff hopes fizzling. Manziel finally got his shot to start at home against Cincinnati on December 14. He was atrocious—10-of-18 for 80 yards with two interceptions in a 30-0 loss. He started the next week at Carolina, where he was pulled in favor of Hoyer after going 3-of-8 for 32 yards in a 17-13 defeat. His off-the-field escapades landed him in rehab soon after the season, but he started six games in 2015. That year he completed 129 of 223 passes for 1,500 yards with seven touchdowns and five interceptions. He also ran the ball 37 times for 230 yards. He was released after the season.

9. c. 774. Incredibly, the Browns lost all four games. Gordon had 125 yards on five receptions, including a 74-yarder for a touchdown from Jason Campbell, in a 41-20 defeat to the Bengals on November 17 in Cincinnati. He had 237 yards on 14 receptions, including a one-yarder for a touchdown from Brandon Weeden, in a 27-11 home loss to Pittsburgh on November 24. He had 261 yards on 10 receptions, including 21- and 95-yarders for touchdowns from Weeden, in a 32-28 home loss to Jacksonville on December 1. He had 151 yards on seven receptions, including an 80-yarder for a touchdown from Campbell, in a 27-26 defeat to the Patriots on December 8 at New England.

Gordon had been selected in the second round of the 2012 supplemental draft. That year, his rookie season, he had 50 receptions for both a team-leading 805 yards and five touchdowns. Despite missing the first two games the next season due to off-the-field issues, he was the team leader in receptions (87), receiving yards (1,646), and touchdown receptions (nine). His yardage total was tops in the entire NFL. In spite of his fantastic 2013 season, which earned him a trip to the Pro Bowl, his off-the-field problems resurfaced and caused him to miss 11 games the next year, got him suspended for the entire 2015 season, and kept him out of the 2016 season.

10. Oakland Raiders. The game would have been at Oakland. The following are the other postseason games the Browns have lost and who they would have played next had they won (NFL Championship games prior to the Super Bowl era, which began in 1966, are not included):

*New York 10, Browns 0 (Eastern Conference Playoff, December 21, 1958, at N.Y.). Had the Browns won . . . vs. Baltimore in the NFL Championship at home

*Dallas 52, Browns 14 (Eastern Conference Championship, December 24, 1967, at Dal.). Had the Browns won . . . at Green Bay in the NFL Championship

*Baltimore 34, Browns 0 (NFL Championship, December 29, 1968, at Cle.). Had the Browns won . . . vs. New York Jets in Super Bowl III at Miami

*Minnesota 27, Browns 7 (NFL Championship, January 4, 1970, at Minn.). Had the Browns won . . . vs. Kansas City in Super Bowl IV at New Orleans

*Baltimore 20, Browns 3 (AFC Divisional Playoff, December 26, 1971, at Cle.). Had the Browns won . . . vs. Miami in the AFC Championship at home

*Miami 20, Browns 14 (AFC Divisional Playoff, December 24, 1972, at Mia.). Had the Browns won . . . at Pittsburgh in the AFC Championship

*Oakland 14, Browns 12 (AFC Divisional Playoff, January 4, 1981, at Cle.). Had the Browns won . . . at San Diego in the AFC Championship

*Los Angeles Raiders 27, Browns 10 (AFC First Round, January 8, 1983, at L.A.). Had the Browns won . . . at Miami in an AFC Second-Round Playoff

*Miami 24, Browns 21 (AFC Divisional Playoff, January 4, 1986, at Mia.). Had the Browns won . . . vs. New England in the AFC Championship at home
*Denver 23, Browns 20 (OT) (AFC Championship, January 11, 1987, at Cle.). Had the Browns won . . . vs. New York Giants in Super Bowl XXI at Pasadena, California
*Denver 38, Browns 33 (AFC Championship, January 17, 1988, at Den.). Had the Browns won . . . vs. Washington in Super Bowl XXII at San Diego
*Houston 24, Browns 23 (AFC Wild Card, December 24, 1988, at Cle.). Had the Browns won . . . at Buffalo in an AFC Divisional Playoff
*Denver 37, Browns 21 (AFC Championship, January 14, 1990, at Den.). Had the Browns won . . . vs. San Francisco in Super Bowl XXIV at New Orleans
*Pittsburgh 29, Browns 9 (AFC Divisional Playoff, January 7, 1995, at Pit.). Had the Browns won . . . at San Diego in the AFC Championship

11. c. December 28, 1969. The Browns beat the Dallas Cowboys 38-14 that afternoon in the Eastern Conference championship game at the Cotton Bowl. Prior to that, they recorded two other road playoff wins—a 38-14 victory over the Rams at Los Angeles in the NFL Championship game on December 26, 1955, and a 14-3 triumph over the Yankees at New York in the AAFC title game on December 14, 1947.

In the win over Dallas, it was all Browns from the start. A two-yard touchdown run by Bo Scott gave them a 7-0 lead after one quarter. They increased their lead to 17-0 at halftime on a six-yard touchdown pass from Bill Nelsen to Milt Morin and a 29-yard field goal by Don Cockroft. Scott scored again from two yards out to make it 24-0 in the third quarter. By the time Leroy Kelly scored from a yard out in the fourth quarter, the Browns were cruising 31-7. Walt Sumner put the icing on the cake when he returned a Craig Morton pass 88 yards for a touchdown to make it 38-7.

Nelsen was 18-of-27 for 219 yards with the touchdown. Kelly rushed the ball 19 times for 66 yards, including a 39-yarder, with the touchdown. Paul Warfield had eight receptions for 99 yards, and Morin caught four passes for 52 yards with the touchdown. Morton was just 8-of-24 for 92 yards with two interceptions. Walt Garrison had nine carries for 49 yards. Bob Hayes had four receptions for 44 yards, while Lance Rentzel had three catches for 41 yards with a touchdown.

12. False. They have played on Turkey Day six times, and all six games were on the road. Their record is 3-3. They defeated the Los Angeles Dons 27-17 on November 27, 1947. They beat the Dons again 31-14 on November 25, 1948. They beat the Chicago Hornets 14-6 on November 24, 1949. The Browns' next Thanksgiving game wasn't until 17 years later when on November 24, 1966, they lost 26-14 to the Dallas Cowboys. Their next one wasn't for 16 years when they fell 31-14 to the Cowboys on November 25, 1982. Their most recent Thanksgiving game was on November 23, 1989, when they lost 13-10 to the Detroit Lions.

The victory over Los Angeles in 1947 was played at the Memorial Coliseum before 45,009 fans. The Dons, who entered 6-6, took an early 10-0 lead before the Browns, who came in 10-1-1, cut the lead to 10-7 after one quarter on a 43-yard touchdown run by Marion Motley. The Browns forged ahead 14-10 at halftime when Otto Graham threw an 18-yard touchdown pass to Tom Colella. They increased their lead to 20-10 after three quarters on a 69-yard scoring strike from Graham to Lew Mayne. The Dons cut the deficit to 20-17 when Glenn Dobbs connected with Chuck Fenenbock on a 35-yard touchdown pass. The final points came when Mac Speedie returned a fumble eight yards for a touchdown.

The 1948 win over Los Angeles was also played at the Memorial Coliseum in front of a crowd of 60,031. Like the year before, the Dons, who entered 7-5, took an early lead, this one 7-0 on a first-quarter, one-yard touchdown run by Walt Clay. The 11-0 Browns tied the game in the second quarter when Graham hooked up with Dante Lavelli for a 49-yard touchdown pass. Clay scored again from a yard out to give the home team a 14-7 lead. The Browns made it 14-all at halftime when Graham hit Bob Cowan on a 17-yard touchdown strike. It was all Browns in the third quarter. First, Graham scored from a yard out to give them their first lead at 21-14. Then Lou Groza booted a 36-yard field goal to make it 24-14. Tony Adamle then scored on a 17-yard touchdown run, and the Browns put it in cruise control the rest of the way.

The triumph over Chicago in 1949 was played at Soldier Field before only 5,031 fans. Two six-yard touchdown runs in the first quarter—one by Bill Boedeker and the other by Marion Motley—gave the 8-1-2 Browns a 14-0 lead. Johnny Clement's one-yard touchdown run in the second quarter put the Hornets, who came in 4-7, on the board, but that is as close as they would come to getting back in the game.

The 1966 defeat to Dallas was played at the Cotton Bowl in front of 80,259 fans. Two Danny Villanueva field goals, from 11 and 31 yards, gave the 7-2-1 Cowboys a 6-0 lead after the first quarter. The Browns, who came in 7-3, sandwiched a one-yard touchdown run by Leroy Kelly and a 16-yard touchdown pass from Frank Ryan to Ernie Green around a short touchdown pass from Don Meredith to Dan Reeves for a 14-13 halftime lead. Two more Villanueva field goals, from 12 and 13 yards, gave Dallas a 19-14 lead after three quarters. A nine-yard touchdown run by Don Perkins shut the door on the Browns.

The loss to Dallas in 1982 was played at Texas Stadium before a crowd of 46,267. After a scoreless first quarter, the 2-1 Cowboys exploded in the second quarter. A short touchdown pass from Danny White to Billy Joe DuPree, a one-yard touchdown run by Tony Dorsett, and a 40-yard field goal by Rafael Septien gave them a 17-0 lead at the half. The home team continued its tear in the third quarter. First, White threw a two-yard touchdown pass to Ron Springs, then Dorsett scored from five yards out to increase the Cowboys' lead to 31-0 entering the fourth quarter. The Browns, who also came in 2-1, avoided the shutout and scored two late touchdowns.

The 1989 defeat to Detroit was played in the Silverdome before 65,624 fans. The Lions, who entered 2-9, took a 3-0 second-quarter lead on a 39-yard field goal by Eddie Murray. The 7-3-1 Browns responded with a 35-yard field goal by Matt Bahr that tied the score. A 27-yard touchdown pass from Bob Gagliano to Richard Johnson put Detroit on top 10-3. Barry Redden ran for a 38-yard touchdown to tie the game at 10 heading to halftime. The only points in the second half came on a 35-yard third-quarter field goal by Murray.

13. Johnny Evans. Whereas Clay and Ozzie were first-rounders, I was taken in the second round out of North Carolina State. As a freshman quarterback for the Wolfpack in 1974, I passed the ball just 23 times, completing nine for 158 yards with a touchdown and four interceptions. I rushed the ball 45 times for 227 yards. I was switched to running back my sophomore year and had 98 carries for 331 yards with three touchdowns. Switched back to quarterback my junior year, I completed 77 of 163 passes for 942 yards with three touchdowns and eight picks. I ran the ball 163 times for 517 yards with seven touchdowns. In my senior year of 1977 I completed 93 of 203 passes for 1,357 yards with eight touchdowns and 10 interceptions. I had 124 rushes for 184 yards with two touchdowns. I also punted the ball 58 times for 2,448 yards. We went 8-4 and I was named MVP of the Peach Bowl in which we defeated Iowa State 24-14.

I was drafted as a punter. In my rookie season of 1978 I punted 78 times for 3,089 yards. The next year I had 69 punts for 2,844 yards, and in our 11-5 AFC Central Division-winning season of 1980, my last, I punted 66 times for 2,530 yards.

14. c. 1969. They finished 10-3-1 that year. The following are the seven home games with attendance figures:

Browns 27, Washington 23 (September 28 – 82,581)
Detroit 28, Browns 21 (October 5 – 82,933)
Browns 42, Pittsburgh 31 (October 18 – 84,078)
Browns 21, St. Louis 21 (October 26 – 81,186)
Browns 42, Dallas 10 (November 2 – 84,850)
Browns 28, New York 17 (November 23 – 80,595)
Browns 20, Green Bay 7 (December 7   82,137)

The following are the other seasons in which the Browns have had at least one home game that drew at least 80,000 fans (number of home games with at least 80,000 fans, number of home games played, and overall record in parentheses):

1947 (1/7 – 12-1-1)
1948 (1/7 – 14-0)
1953 (1/6 – 11-1)
1961 (1/7 – 8-5-1)
1962 (2/7 – 7-6-1)
1963 (2/7 – 10-4)
1964 (3/7 – 10-3-1)
1965 (5/7 – 11-3)
1966 (3/7 – 9-5)
1967 (3/7 – 9-5)
1968 (3/7 – 10-4)
1970 (5/7 – 7-7)
1971 (3/7 – 9-5)
1972 (3/7 – 10-4)
1977 (1/7 – 6-8)
1978 (1/8 – 8-8)
1979 (3/8 – 9-7)
1980 (3/8 – 11-5)

15. b. Seattle, San Francisco. The Browns were embarrassed 33-0 by the Seahawks at Seattle in their season opener on Monday, September 3. They were destroyed at home 41-7 by the 49ers on November 11. The Seattle game was supposed to have been played the day before, but a scheduling conflict with the Seattle Mariners pushed the game back a day. The Seahawks took a 7-0 first-quarter lead on a five-yard touchdown pass from Dave Krieg to Mike Tice. In the second quarter a seven-yard touchdown pass from Krieg to Paul Johns was sandwiched between two field goals by Norm Johnson for a 20-0 Seattle halftime lead. Two more Johnson field goals—41- and 24-yarders—upped the home team's lead to 26-0 after three quarters. Krieg hit Daryl Turner on a 34-yard touchdown pass for the final points.

Seattle dominated Cleveland 307-120 in total yards. Paul McDonald was 8-of-27 for 114 yards with two interceptions and was sacked five times. Duriel Harris had two receptions for 45 yards, including a 32-yarder from McDonald. Krieg was 14-of-28 for 179 yards with the three touchdowns and an interception; he was sacked twice. Johns had three catches for 49 yards, including a 32-yarder from Krieg, with the touchdown, while Pete Metzelaars caught three balls for 46 yards.

Against the 49ers, who were 9-1, the 2-8 Browns were completely outclassed. Two Ray Wersching field goals in the first quarter and a 20-yard touchdown run by Roger Craig in the second quarter gave San Francisco a 13-0 halftime lead. Then the 49ers really put the pedal to the metal. Craig scored from two yards out, and Joe Montana threw a 60-yard touchdown pass to Freddie Solomon for a 27-0 lead after three quarters. Montana and Solomon hooked up again, this time for a two-yard touchdown strike, and Bill Ring scored on a five-yard touchdown run for a 41-0 Niners advantage. The Browns avoided the shutout when Bruce Davis caught an 18-yard touchdown pass from McDonald.

San Francisco dominated the Browns 213-43 in rushing yards and 468-251 in total yards. McDonald was 13-of-33 for 220 yards with the touchdown and an interception; he was sacked twice. Davis had four receptions for 64 yards with the touchdown. Ozzie Newsome had two catches for 56 yards, including a 47-yarder from McDonald, and Brian Brennan had a 52-yard reception from McDonald. Montana was 24-of-30 for 263 yards with the two touchdowns and a pick; he was sacked once. Wendell Tyler rushed the ball 17 times for 87 yards. Ring had six rushes for 48 yards, including a 34-yarder, with the touchdown. Craig ran the ball nine times for 45 yards with the two touchdowns and had eight receptions for 49 yards. Solomon had five catches for 105 yards with the two touchdowns.

16. c. 16. They are Otto Graham, Paul Brown, Marion Motley, Jim Brown, Lou Groza, Dante Lavelli, Len Ford, Bill Willis, Bobby Mitchell, Paul Warfield, Mike McCormack, Frank Gatski, Leroy Kelly, Ozzie Newsome, Joe DeLamielleure, and Gene Hickerson. The following are bios of each player with the year they were inducted:

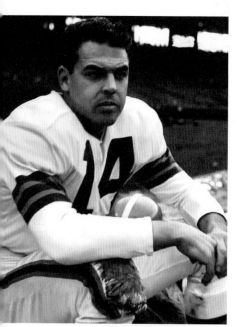

Otto Graham. (AndersonsCle-velandDesign.com)

*Otto Graham (1965) -Graham was a quarterback from 1946-55. As a free agent, he was the first player ever signed by the Browns. He led them to all four AAFC championships from 1946-49 and to all six NFL title games, winning three of them, from 1950-55. He was a Pro Bowler from 1950-54. He passed for a then team-record

23,584 yards. He retired after the 1955 season. Graham's uniform number 14 is retired (he also wore number 60).

*Paul Brown (1967)

-Brown was Cleveland's first head coach. He held the position from 1946-62. His surname is the reason behind the team's nickname; he is the only pro football coach for whom a team has been named. He led the Browns to four straight AAFC championships from 1946-49 and six straight NFL title-game appearances from 1950-55, winning in 1950 and from 1954-55. He was fired by Art Modell on January 9, 1963. His all-time record was 158-48-8.

*Marion Motley (1968)

-Motley was a running back from 1946-53. He signed as a free agent. Motley led the team in rushing yards every season from 1946-50 and in 1952, rushing for 4,172 yards overall. Most of them came in the AAFC, of which he is the all-time rushing leader with 3,024 yards. He was a Pro Bowler in 1950. He retired in 1954 but then attempted a comeback as a linebacker and on September 8, 1955, was traded to the Pittsburgh Steelers.

*Jim Brown (1971)

-Brown was a fullback from 1957-65. He was a first-round draft choice in 1957 out of Syracuse University. He rushed for 1,000 yards in seven of his nine seasons and was the team leader in that category every year, including a franchise-record 1,863 in 1963. He was a Pro Bowler all nine years. Overall, Brown rushed for a team-record 12,312 yards and averaged an NFL-record 104.3 yards per game and 5.2 yards per carry. He retired in the summer of 1966 to pursue an acting career in the movies. His uniform number 32 is retired.

Jim Brown in action against the Cowboys, 1964. (The Cleveland Press Collection, Michael Schwartz Library, Cleveland State University)

*Lou Groza (1974)
-Groza signed as a free agent. He was an offensive lineman and kicker from 1946-59. He retired for one season—1960—due

172

to a back injury during training camp. Upon his return in 1961, he focused solely on his kicking duties. He was picked for the Pro Bowl from 1950-55 and 1957-59. Groza is the Browns' all-time leading scorer with 1,608 points. He retired in 1968. His uniform number 76 is retired (he also wore number 46).

*Dante Lavelli (1975)

-Lavelli was a wide receiver from 1946-56. He signed as a free agent. He led the Browns in receptions in 1946, 1951, and from 1953-54; in receiving yards in 1946, 1950, and 1953; and in touchdown receptions from 1946-47, in 1951, and from 1953-54. Lavelli was chosen for the Pro Bowl in 1951 and from 1953-54. Overall, he totaled 386 receptions, 6,488 receiving yards, and 62 touchdown catches. He retired after the 1956 season.

*Len Ford (1976)

-Ford was a defensive end from 1950-57. He was an early-round choice from the University of Michigan in the 1950 special allocation draft that consisted of players (other than those from the New York Yankees, who were split among the New York Giants and New York Bulldogs) from the folded AAFC. He was a Pro Bowler from 1951-54. Ford totaled 19 fumble recoveries, including one that he returned 54 yards against the Eagles on November 13, 1955. He was traded to the Packers in May 1958.

*Bill Willis (1977)

-Willis was a defensive lineman from 1946-53. He signed as a free agent. Willis saved the day in an 8-3 victory over the New York Giants in an American Conference playoff on December 17, 1950, in Cleveland when late in the game he tackled fullback Gene Roberts from behind at the Browns' four-yard line. He was selected to play in the Pro Bowl from 1950-52 and retired after the 1953 season.

*Bobby Mitchell (1983)
-Mitchell was a running back from 1958-61. He was a seventh-round draft choice in 1958 from the University of Illinois. He complemented Brown well, finishing second on the team to him in rushing yards all four seasons. Mitchell ran for 232 yards, including a 90-yarder for a touchdown, on November 15, 1959, against the Redskins. He led the Browns with 45 receptions in 1960 and also led the team in punt returns in 1959, punt return yards from 1958-59, kickoff returns from 1958-60, and kickoff return yards all four years. He returned both three punts and three kickoffs for touchdowns. Mitchell was a Pro Bowler in 1960. He was traded to Washington on December 4, 1961, the day of the 1962 NFL Draft, but did not join the Redskins until the 1962 season.
*Paul Warfield (1983)
-Warfield was a wide receiver from 1964-69 and 1976-77. He was a first-round draft choice in 1964 from Ohio State University. Warfield averaged an incredible 20.7 yards per catch from 1964-69, before he was traded to Miami on January 26, 1970, for the Dolphins' first-round pick in the next day's draft. The Browns made the trade in order to draft Purdue University quarterback Mike Phipps. Warfield was re-signed in 1976 after five playoff seasons—including two Super Bowl Championships—with the Dolphins and one season in the WFL. He totaled 5,210 receiving yards. He was picked for the Pro Bowl in 1964 and from 1968-69. He retired after the 1977 season.
*Mike McCormack (1984)
-McCormack was mainly an offensive tackle from 1954-62. He was traded from Baltimore on March 26, 1953. McCormack was an integral part of offensive lines that paved the way for

Brown and Mitchell. He was picked for the Pro Bowl from 1956-57 and 1960-62 and retired after the 1962 season.

*Frank Gatski (1985)

-Gatski was a center from 1946-56. He signed as a free agent. Gatski was a key cog to offensive lines that helped protect Graham and blocked for Motley. He was picked to play in the Pro Bowl in 1956 before being traded to the Detroit Lions after the 1956 season.

*Leroy Kelly (1994)

-Kelly was a running back from 1964-73. He was an eighth-round draft pick in 1964 from Morgan State University. Kelly led Cleveland in rushing yards every season from 1966-72 and earned three straight 1,000-yard rushing seasons from 1966-68. Overall, he ran for 7,274 yards with 74 touchdowns and had 190 receptions for 2,281 receiving yards with 13 touchdowns. He also totaled 990 punt return yards with three touchdowns and 1,784 kickoff return yards. He was a Pro Bowl selection from 1966-71. He was released prior to the 1974 season.

*Ozzie Newsome (1999)

-Newsome was a tight end from 1978-90. He was a first-round draft choice in 1978 from the University of Alabama. He led the Browns in receptions and receiving yards every season from 1981-85 and in touchdown receptions in 1979, 1981, and from 1983-85. Overall, his 662 receptions rank first in team annals, as do his 7,980 career receiving yards. Newsome was a Pro Bowler in 1981 and from 1984-85. He retired after the 1990 season.

*Joe DeLamielleure (2003)

-DeLamielleure was a guard from 1980-84. He was traded from Buffalo on September 1, 1980. DeLamielleure was an integral

Ozzie Newsome makes a one-handed catch for a 14-yard touchdown as Miami's Norris Thomas hangs on in the Browns' 30-24 overtime win, November 18, 1979. (The Cleveland Press Collection, Michael Schwartz Library, Cleveland State University)

part of offensive lines that protected Brian Sipe in 1980 and paved the way for three 1,000-yard rushing seasons for Mike Pruitt. He was voted to the Pro Bowl in 1980.

*Gene Hickerson (2007)

-Hickerson was a guard from 1958-60 and 1962-73. He was a seventh-round draft choice in 1957 from the University of Mississippi with one year of eligibility in school left. He missed the 1961 season due to a broken leg suffered in the first preseason game and subsequently fractured the same leg again late in the year while watching a game from the sideline. Hickerson was a key cog to offensive lines that blocked for Brown and Kelly. He was a Pro Bowler from 1965-70.

In addition to the aforementioned Hall of Famers, the following are five Hall of Fame players who spent part of their playing careers with the Browns:

Doug Atkins (1953-54)
Henry Jordan (1957-58)
Willie Davis (1958-59)
Len Dawson (1960-61)
Tommy McDonald (1968)

The following two Hall of Famers, inducted as coaches, spent part of their playing careers with the Browns:

Don Shula (1951-52)
Chuck Noll (1953-59)

17. Paul McDonald made his first start at home against the Pittsburgh Steelers on December 19, 1982. Mike Phipps started his first game against the Bengals in Cincinnati on November 15, 1970. Brian Sipe made his first start against the Chargers in San Diego on November 3, 1974. Bernie Kosar started his first game against the Oilers at Houston on October 13, 1985.

A fourth-round draft pick in 1980 out of USC, McDonald had backed up Sipe for two-and-a-half seasons. In his start against Pittsburgh, the 2-4 Browns took a 3-0 first-quarter lead on a 44-yard field goal by Matt Bahr. The 4-2 Steelers took a 7-3 halftime lead when Terry Bradshaw hit John Stallworth on a six-yard touchdown pass in the second quarter. The Browns forged back ahead 10-7 in the third quarter on a one-yard touchdown run by Johnny Davis. Steve Cox ran out of the end zone to give Pittsburgh a fourth-quarter safety, and the Browns hung on to win 10-9.

McDonald was 19-of-40 for 227 yards with an interception and was sacked six times. Dwight Walker had four receptions for 57 yards, including a 31-yarder from McDonald. Dave Logan had four catches for 52 yards. Bradshaw was 12-of-39 for 144 yards with the touchdown and four interceptions, three by Hanford Dixon; he was sacked three times. Franco Harris rushed the ball 14 times for 65 yards and caught three passes for 24 yards. Jim Smith had four catches for 74 yards, including a 35-yarder from Bradshaw.

A first-round draft selection in 1970 from Purdue University, Phipps had backed up Bill Nelsen that season. In his start against Cincinnati, the Browns, who came in 4-4, took a 7-0 lead in the first quarter when Leroy Kelly scored from nine yards out. They upped their lead to 10-0 in the second quarter on a Don Cockroft 15-yard field goal. The Bengals, who entered 2-6, made it 10-7 at halftime on a 13-yard touchdown pass from Virgil Carter to Jess Phillips. Paul Robinson's one-yard touchdown run in the third quarter was the winning points in Cincinnati's 14-10 triumph.

Phipps was 11-of-25 for 170 yards with an interception. He also ran the ball four times for 57 yards. Kelly carried the ball 21 times for 60 yards with the touchdown. Milt Morin had three receptions for 78 yards. Carter was 10-of-17 for 123 yards with the touchdown. He also ran the ball nine times for 110 yards. Robinson had 14 rushes for 63 yards with the touchdown, while Chip Myers had three receptions for 67 yards.

A 13th-round draft choice in 1972 from San Diego State University, Sipe had spent two seasons on the taxi squad and then had backed up Phipps for the first half of the 1974 season. In Sipe's start against San Diego, the Browns, who entered 2-5, took a 14-0 first-quarter lead on a short touchdown pass from Sipe to Steve Holden and a short touchdown run by Greg Pruitt. They were up 21-7 in the third quarter, but the 1-6 Chargers cut their deficit to 21-19 on two Dan Fouts touchdown passes entering the fourth quarter. Two Browns touchdowns sandwiched a 70-yard scoring strike from Fouts to Harrison Davis, and Cleveland was up 35-26. Fouts hit Don Woods for a 75-yard scoring strike to cut it to 35-33. Ray Wersching's 40-yard field goal was the winning points in San Diego's wild 36-35 victory.

Sipe was 16-of-23 for 186 yards with the touchdown and an interception. Greg Pruitt had 17 carries for 47 yards with the touchdown and had three receptions for 38 yards. Holden had six catches for 85 yards with the touchdown. Fouts was 12-of-21 for 333 yards with the four touchdowns and a pick. Woods rushed the ball 18 times for 51 yards and had three receptions for 119 yards with two touchdowns. Davis had four receptions for 142 yards with the touchdown, and Gary Garrison caught three passes for 68 yards.

A first-round pick in the 1985 supplemental draft out of the University of Miami, Kosar had backed up Gary Danielson that season until the veteran got injured during a Week 5 win over New England. In Kosar's start the next week against Houston, the Oilers, who came in 1-4, led 6-0 at halftime on two Tony Zendejas field goals. The Browns, who entered 3-2, took a 7-6 lead in the third quarter when Kosar hit Clarence Weathers on a 68-yard touchdown pass. A four-yard touchdown run by Kevin Mack later in the third and a five-yard touchdown run by Earnest Byner in the fourth quarter gave Cleveland a 21-6 victory.

Kosar was 8-of-19 for 208 yards with the touchdown and an interception. Mack ran the ball 20 times for 91 yards with the touchdown, and Byner had 14 carries for 54 yards with the touchdown and two receptions for 18 yards. Weathers had three receptions for 146 yards with the touchdown, while Brian Brennan had two catches for 37 yards. Warren Moon was 14-of-23 for 97 yards with a pick and was sacked five times. He ran the ball three times for 19 yards. Mike Rozier rushed the ball 16 times for 49 yards. Drew Hill had four receptions for 48 yards, and Butch Woolfolk had eight catches for 46 yards.

18. New England Patriots. Other than returning kickoffs and punts, Feacher had seen little action when he came off the bench in the Bengals game. With the Browns, who came in 10-5, trailing 10-0 in the second quarter, Brian Sipe threw a 42-yard touchdown pass to Reggie Rucker to make it 10-7. Don Cockroft's 26-yard field goal tied the score 10-10 at halftime. Ray Griffin intercepted a Sipe pass and returned it 52 yards for a touchdown to give Cincinnati, which entered 6-9, a 17-10 third-quarter lead. Soon after, Feacher caught a 35-yard touchdown pass from Sipe to tie the game. Then, Feacher did it again—this time he was on the receiving end of a 34-yard scoring strike from Sipe to give the Browns their first lead at 24-17.

Pat McInally, the victim of a vicious hit by Thom Darden earlier in the game, made a spectacular play on a 59-yard touchdown catch from Jack Thompson to make it 24-24 heading to the fourth quarter. Cockroft's 22-yard field goal late in the game gave Cleveland the lead again. The Bengals were driving well into Browns territory, but luckily for the visitors, time ran out on them.

Sipe was 24-of-44 for 308 yards with the three touchdowns and two interceptions. Mike Pruitt had 14 rushes for 51 yards.

Rucker had four receptions for 74 yards with the touchdown. Dave Logan caught a single pass for 65 yards. Thompson was 12-of-30 for 197 yards with the touchdown and two picks. Charles Alexander had eight carries for 50 yards, including a 32-yarder. McInally had three receptions for 86 yards with the touchdown. Dan Ross caught five passes for 77 yards, including a 34-yarder, and Steve Kreider had three catches for 54 yards.

19. False. They have played one tie game in that period, a 10-10 deadlock with visiting Kansas City on November 19, 1989. They played to a dozen ties prior to 1974. The first was 28-28 against the Yankees on November 23, 1947, in New York. The last was 20-20 against the Chiefs on December 2, 1973, at Kansas City.

The 1989 game against the Chiefs was scoreless until Matt Bahr connected on a 40-yard field goal in the second quarter to give the 7-3 Browns a 3-0 halftime lead. Kansas City, which entered 4-6, took a 7-3 lead in the third quarter when Neil Smith returned Mike Oliphant's fumble three yards for a touchdown. Eric Metcalf's short touchdown run gave Cleveland a 10-7 lead entering the fourth quarter. Nick Lowery's 41-yard field goal with 3:48 remaining tied the score. Lowery, one of the most accurate kickers in NFL history, was wide right on a 45-yarder with four seconds left in regulation, but an offside penalty against the Browns gave him a second chance from 39 yards. That one was wide left. He was short on a 47-yard try with three seconds to go in overtime.

Bernie Kosar was 21-of-42 for 198 yards with an interception and was sacked three times. Webster Slaughter caught six passes for 67 yards. Tim Manoa had three receptions for 41 yards, including a 32-yarder from Kosar, and rushed the ball 13 times for 34 yards. Steve DeBerg was 17-of-40 for 209 yards with two picks; he was sacked three times. Herman Heard rushed the ball seven times for 35 yards, including a 28-yarder, and had three receptions for 40 yards, including a 25-yarder from DeBerg. Pete Mandley had four receptions for 56 yards.

20. Tom Bloom and Don Fleming. The Browns had acquired Davis, a halfback, three days prior to their 1961 season finale by trading Bobby Mitchell and the rights to number-two draft choice Leroy Jackson to Washington for the Redskins' first-round selection, which was the top pick in the draft, Davis. Davis had speed and power as a running back that helped him break most of Jim Brown's records at Syracuse University.

In 1959, for the 11-0 National Champion Orangemen, Davis rushed the ball 98 times for a team-leading 686 yards and had 11 receptions for 94 yards. The next season he ran the ball 112 times for 877 yards with eight touchdowns, all of which were team highs. He also had 11 receptions for 141 yards with a team-leading two touchdowns. In 1961 he carried the ball 150 times for 823 yards with 12 touchdowns, all of which were team bests. He also had a team-leading 16 catches for 157 yards with two touchdowns. Unfortunately, tragedy struck as Davis contracted leukemia and never played a game for the Browns. He passed away on May 18, 1963.

About two weeks after Davis passed on, standout defensive back Don Fleming was electrocuted on a construction project in Florida. Fleming had begun what looked to be a promising career in the NFL. In his rookie season of 1960 he had five interceptions and a fumble recovery. In 1961 he had three interceptions and two fumble recoveries, and in 1963 he had two picks and a fumble recovery.

Some five months earlier, Bloom, a sixth-round draft pick in 1963 who was a three-year running back for Purdue University, was killed in an automobile accident. He was mainly a backup for the Boilermakers in 1960. In 1961 he rushed the ball 38 times for 236 yards with a touchdown and had 14 receptions for 128 yards. In 1962 he ran the ball 43 times for 192 yards and had a team-leading 13 catches for a team-best 217 yards with two touchdowns. Bloom, who had hoped to win a spot in Cleveland's defensive backfield, was driving the car he had purchased with the bonus money he had received for signing with the Browns.

21. 1946 and 1948. They defeated the Seahawks 34-0 on December 3, 1946, and beat the Colts 14-10 on October 5, 1948. In the Miami game, the 10-2 Browns dominated from the start. Nine turnovers by the 2-9 Seahawks helped. Otto Graham, playing defensive back, returned an interception 37 yards for a touchdown to give the Browns a 7-0 lead after the first quarter. A short touchdown run by Edgar Jones and a 50-yard field goal by Lou Groza increased their lead to 17-0 at halftime. Gaylon Smith's two-yard touchdown run upped the lead to 24-0 after three quarters. The Browns' lead ballooned even more on an 11-yard Groza field goal and a 16-yard touchdown run by Gene Fekete, the game's final points.

Against Baltimore, the Colts, who entered 3-1, took a 7-0 first-quarter lead on a 78-yard touchdown pass from Y.A. Tittle to Billy Hillenbrand. The 4-0 Browns tied the score after one quarter when Jones scored from two yards out. Baltimore took a 10-7 halftime lead on a 40-yard field goal by Rex Grossman. In the third quarter Jones scored again, this time on a 12-yard pass from Graham for the game's final points. Marion Motley rushed for 130 yards.

22. c. 15. The following are the dates and names of those who appeared:

October 8, 1956	Paul Brown, George Ratterman
September 26, 1960	Jim Brown
January 4, 1965	Frank Ryan
September 27, 1965	Frank Ryan
November 21, 1966	Ross Fichtner
September 8, 1980	Dave Logan
August 30, 1982	Tom Cousineau
August 26, 1985	Bernie Kosar
January 12, 1987	Ozzie Newsome
August 29, 1988	Bernie Kosar
December 4, 1995	Art Modell
April 19, 1999	Big Dawg (superfan), Tim Couch, Akili Smith (never played for the Browns)
September 1, 1999	Jim Brown, Tim Couch (special commemorative issue honoring the return of the Browns to the NFL after three seasons without NFL football in Cleveland)
August 6, 2007	Jamal Lewis
May 19, 2014	Johnny Manziel

23. Tom Tupa. The former Ohio State University punter and quarterback (the latter for one season) turned the trick in the 1994 season opener on September 4 at Cincinnati. With the Browns leading 9-0 in the first quarter, Tupa, the holder on an extra-point attempt following an 11-yard touchdown pass from Vinny Testaverde to Leroy Hoard, took the snap and charged up the middle and into the end zone to increase the Browns' lead to 11-0. In the second quarter the Bengals sandwiched a short touchdown run by Derrick Fenner and a 38-yard field goal by Doug Pelfrey around two huge special teams touchdowns by Cleveland. The first was an 85-yard kickoff return by Randy Baldwin; the second was a 92-yard punt return by Eric Metcalf. The Browns led 25-10 at the half en route to a 28-20 victory.

Testaverde was 14-of-24 for 149 yards with the touchdown and two interceptions. Hoard ran the ball 16 times for 92 yards and had the receiving touchdown. Michael Jackson had three receptions for 45 yards. David Klingler was 27-of-43 for 224 yards with a touchdown and two picks; he was sacked twice. Steve Broussard had six rushes for 48 yards and six receptions for 35 yards. Fenner had 13 carries for 41 yards with the touchdown and seven catches for 60 yards. Darnay Scott caught three passes for 50 yards with a touchdown.

As for Tupa, who had five punts for 200 yards against the Bengals, he had been signed as a free agent in 1994 and punted for the Browns through the next season.

24. c. Four. Jim Brown won the NFL award in 1957 by the Associated Press, United Press, and *The Sporting News*. Bobby Mitchell won the NFL award in 1958 by *The Sporting News*. Chip Banks won the NFL defensive honor in 1982 by the Associated Press and *Pro Football Weekly*. Kevin Mack won the AFC accolade in 1985 by United Press International. All but Mitchell were Pro Bowlers in their respective rookie seasons.

Brown, a fullback and a first-round choice in the 1957 draft out of Syracuse University, rushed for both a team-leading 942 yards and nine touchdowns on a team-high 202 carries. He also had 16 receptions for 55 yards with a touchdown. He only had two games in which he gained 100 yards or more, but one of them was a 237-yard performance in a 45-31 win over the visiting Los Angeles Rams on November 24. He did it on 31 carries, which included four touchdowns, one of which was a season-long 69-yarder in the second quarter that gave the Browns a 14-7 lead. With Cleveland trailing 28-17, he ran for three short touchdowns in a row in the third and fourth quarters to give his team a 38-28 lead it would not relinquish. He also had three catches for 21 yards. His other game in which he topped the century mark was three weeks earlier, on November 3, when he rushed for 109 yards on 21 carries with two touchdowns in a 21-17 victory over Washington, also at home. He also returned six kickoffs for 136 yards. In a 59-14 loss at Detroit in the NFL Championship game on December 29, he rushed the ball 20 times for 69 yards with a touchdown and returned four kickoffs for 106 yards.

Mitchell, a running back and a seventh-round selection in the 1958 draft from the University of Illinois, had 80 rushes for 500 yards. He also had 16 receptions for 131 yards with three touchdowns. He had two games in which he ran for 100 yards. The first was a 35-28 win over the visiting Cardinals on October 12 when he gained 147 yards on the ground on 11 carries, including a 63-yard touchdown run, his only touchdown run of the season. A week later, on October 19, in a 27-10 triumph over Pittsburgh, also at home, he had 13 rushes for 108 yards, including a 35-yarder, and caught three passes for 38 yards, including a seven-yarder for a touchdown from Milt Plum. He was also used as a kickoff and punt returner. Mitchell had both a team-leading 18 kickoff returns and 454 kickoff return yards, including a 98-yarder for a touchdown in the first quarter of a 28-14 home victory over Philadelphia on November 23. Later in the same quarter he returned a punt

68 yards for a touchdown, one of 14 punt returns he had that season for a team-high 165 yards.

Banks, a left outside linebacker and a 1982 first-round draft selection from USC, had a nose for the football. He was . . . well . . . everywhere. He may have only had 5.5 sacks, albeit the most on the team, but he was a game changer with what seemed like an infinite number of quarterback pressures. He made quite an impression in the season opener in the form of three sacks of Dave Krieg that helped the Browns to a 21-7 triumph. He also notched a sack of Ken Anderson in a loss at Cincinnati on December 12 and had 1.5 sacks of Gifford Nielsen in a crucial victory at Houston on December 26. A week later in a season-ending loss at Pittsburgh, he intercepted a Terry Bradshaw pass and returned it 14 yards.

Mack, a fullback and a 1984 first-round supplemental draft pick out of Clemson University, rushed for a team-best 1,104 yards with seven touchdowns on 222 carries. He also caught 29 passes for 297 yards with three touchdowns. His breakout game came in a 21-7 Week 4 win at San Diego in which he totaled 130 yards rushing on 16 carries, including a season-long 61-yard jaunt and a 10-yard touchdown run. He also caught seven passes for 49 yards, including a 10-yard touchdown pass from Gary Danielson. The next week in a 24-20 home victory over New England he had 20 carries for 115 yards, including a 10-yard touchdown run in the fourth quarter that turned out to be the winning points. He also had five receptions for 85 yards. His other 100-yard game was on November 24 in a crucial 24-6 triumph over the visiting Bengals. He rushed for 117 yards on 14 carries, including 2 and 35 yard touchdown runs. He had 13 rushes for 56 yards in a 24-21 divisional playoff loss to the Dolphins in Miami on January 4.

25. Brian Sipe had 26 touchdown passes in 1983, Bill Nelsen had 23 touchdown passes in 1969, Bernie Kosar had 17 touchdown passes in 1986, and Derek Anderson had 29 touchdown passes in 2007. Nelsen and Anderson earned their only Pro Bowl appearances in their respective seasons.

Sipe rebounded big time in 1983 after going from being "All-World" in 1980 to being benched during the 1982 season. Besides his 26 touchdown passes in 1983, he also completed 291 of 496 passes for 3,566 yards; he had 23 interceptions, too. Paul McDonald did start in his place midway through the season when he was struggling, but only for two games. In a 31-26 win over the Lions at Detroit in Week 2, Sipe was 18-of-29 for 234 yards with four touchdowns. Two weeks later, in a 30-24 overtime win at San Diego, he was 27-of-44 for 327 yards with three touchdowns, including the game-winning 48-yarder to Harry Holt. In a 41-23 victory over visiting Baltimore on November 27, he was 20-of-33 for 313 yards with three touchdowns, including a 66-yarder to Ozzie Newsome. Three weeks later in the season finale on December 18, in his final NFL game, he was 14-of-22 for 199 yards with four touchdowns in leading his team to a 30-17 home triumph over Pittsburgh.

To go with his 23 touchdown passes in 1969, Nelsen completed 190 of 352 passes for 2,743 yards with 19 interceptions. By far, his best game was a 42-10 rout of the visiting Dallas Cowboys on November 2 in which he was 18-of-25 for 255 yards with five touchdowns and one interception. In a Week 4 win at New Orleans he was 15-of-25 for 214 yards with a touchdown. On November 30 at Wrigley Field, he was

16-of-30 for 290 yards with two touchdowns in a 28-24 victory over the Bears. In a 38-14 rout of the Cowboys at the Cotton Bowl in the Eastern Conference championship game, he was 18-of-27 for 219 yards with a touchdown. In a 27-7 loss at Minnesota the next week in the NFL title game, he was 17-of-33 for 181 yards with a touchdown and two picks.

In 1986, Kosar completed 310 of 531 passes for 3,854 yards with 10 interceptions to go with his 17 touchdown passes. He had two 400-yard games. The first was a 26-16 Monday night victory over the visiting Dolphins on November 10 when he was 32-of-50 for 401 yards. The second was two weeks later, on November 23 in a 37-31 overtime win at home against the Steelers when he was 28-of-46 for 414 yards with an interception and two touchdowns, including the game-winning 36-yard strike to Webster Slaughter. Two other great performances he had were road wins over Pittsburgh and Indianapolis. In a 27-24 triumph over the Steelers on October 5—the Browns' first-ever win in Three Rivers Stadium in 17 tries—he was 14-of-23 for 186 yards with a touchdown. In a 24-9 victory over the Colts on November 2, he was 15-of-25 for 238 yards with three touchdowns. He had a performance for the ages in an AFC Divisional Playoff in which he was 33-of-64 for 489 yards—still an NFL playoff record—with a touchdown and two picks in a 23-20 double-overtime triumph over the visiting New York Jets. In a 23-20 overtime loss at home to Denver the next week in the AFC title game—"The Drive" contest—he was 18-of-32 for 259 yards with two touchdowns and two interceptions.

Anderson's 2007 season was what one would call a "one-season wonder" after he replaced the soon-to-be-traded Charlie Frye during the season opener at home against Pittsburgh. To go with his 29 touchdown passes, he completed 298 of 527 passes for 3,787 yards with 19 interceptions. Starting with a 20-of-33, 328-yard, five-touchdown pass, one-interception performance in a Week 2 51-45 win at home over the Bengals, he enjoyed a tremendous season, especially the first half. In consecutive October wins over Miami and St. Louis, respectively, he was 18-of-25 with three touchdowns in each game, passing for 245 yards against the Dolphins and 248 against the Rams. A week later in a 33-30 overtime win at home against Seattle, he was 29-of-48 for 364 yards with an interception. Unfortunately, his dreadful performance in a 19-14 loss at Cincinnati on December 23 in the next-to-last game is what he will be remembered for by many fans. He was 29-of-48 for 251 yards with two touchdowns but also four interceptions, two of which came on consecutive passes that led to Bengals touchdowns late in the first half. The defeat wound up costing the Browns a playoff berth.

EXTRA POINT

It's over. You're done. You did it! Now you are officially an authority on Cleveland Browns history. To celebrate your new-found expertise, how about one for the road? Here's one last brainteaser that will, in all likelihood, knock your orange and brown socks off.

QUESTION:
Of the AFC franchises that were in existence when ABC Monday Night Football *began, which is the only one the Browns have never played on MNF?*

ANSWER:
Kansas City Chiefs. If you correctly answered this tricky bit of Browns trivia, perhaps you, not I, should have written this book.

ACKNOWLEDGMENTS

I would like to thank Niels Aaboe of Skyhorse Publishing for giving me the opportunity to write this book, and everyone else there, especially Julie Ganz, for their assistance. I would also like to thank AndersonsClevelandDesign.com and The Cleveland Press Collection in the Michael Schwartz Library at Cleveland State University for providing photos. Special thanks to Thom Darden for writing the foreword.